SENSIBLE JOB INTERVIEWING

Understanding The Employer's Role & Responsibilities

S.H.C. Owen M.Ed.

Bloomington, IN   Milton Keynes, UK

AuthorHouse™
1663 Liberty Drive, Suite 200
Bloomington, IN 47403
www.authorhouse.com
Phone: 1-800-839-8640

AuthorHouse™ UK Ltd.
500 Avebury Boulevard
Central Milton Keynes, MK9 2BE
www.authorhouse.co.uk
Phone: 08001974150

©2006 S.H.C. Owen M.Ed.. All rights reserved.

No part of this book may be reproduced, stored in a retrieval system, or transmitted by any means without the written permission of the author.

First published by AuthorHouse 12/13/2006

ISBN: 978-1-4259-6194-7 (sc)

Library of Congress Control Number: 1425961940

Printed in the United States of America
Bloomington, Indiana

This book is printed on acid-free paper.

Visit the author's website:
http://sensiblejobinterviewing.com

Table of Contents

Preface	VII
Introduction	1
1 Why Employment?	15
Employment's Purpose	15
Organizational Commitment and Dedication	18
Thought Conformity	19
Personality Judgments	21
Attitudes	24
Morale	26
2 Business Sense	29
The Work	29
Business Teaming	31
Business Compliance	33
Business Clarity	34
Business Expectations	37
3 Interviewer Concerns	41
Interviewer's Abilities	44
Interpersonal Communications	45
Irrelevancies	47
Biases	48
Comprehension	49
Structured Interview Types	51
4 Preparing Interview Content	55
Process Elements	56
Role Play	56
Defining Expectations	57
Clarifying Objectives	58
Crafting the Position Profile	61
Evaluating the Position Profile	62
5 Talent and Bumps in the Dark	65
Types of Knowledge	66
Intelligence and Creativity	67
Thinking	68
Types of Reasoning	71
Beliefs	72

6 Applicant Beware	75
Projected Image	75
Finding the Image	76
Motivation	78
Harsh Realities	84
7 Applicant Controls	87
Picking Destination(s)	87
Mapping Terrain	88
Higher Octane Fuel	92
Lower Octane Fuel	92
Know Business's Intent	93
8 Session Essentials	97
Interview Scheduling Procedures	97
Session's Intent	100
Applicant Responsiveness	101
Critical Thinking Conditions	102
A Connective Interview Session	105
Connective's Purpose	110
Applicant's Connective Ratings	111
Scoring Responses	112
9 Putting It All Together	115
Employer's Three Determinants	115
Connective's Improvements	118
Case Study	121
Tying Loose Ends	124
Summary Thoughts	126
Afterthought	133
References by Chapter	145
Index	153

Preface

Like turning a doorknob, job interviewing is a familiar and essential business convention that too often is taken for granted. An employer has need of a worker, and various individuals seek an employment opportunity through that business's entryway. What happens when a latch doesn't work properly? The door opens with a little effort, unnecessary difficulty, or not at all, regardless of one's capability and best intentions. Both employer and applicant still grab the knob, twisting back and forth, urgently tugging and pushing to make a business connection because it appears okay. The well-known job interview has the appearance of functioning properly and perhaps in the past worked fine. But unseen parts, like the internal parts of an old door's latch, have become so badly worn and misaligned that it is no longer able to work, as it should most of the time. This creates inconveniences and lost business opportunities not only for those invitees, known as job applicants, but also for their hosts. In short, employers should replace their traditional job interviewing practices by installing a newer, more secure, and more reliable means for handling this critical business function. This book explains to employers in detail why this change is necessary and demonstrates how to proceed. Individuals looking for employment now or in the future will learn how to manipulate outdated interviewing methods more adeptly and how to best prepare for the new interviewing process that wise employers will be implementing.

During almost thirty-five years of varied employment, I have had experiences on both sides of the interview table. On the applicant's, or weaker, side of the table, I confess that whether I was successful or not in obtaining an offer of employment had everything to do with my interview performance or projected image. Yet, I cannot recall one instance as an employee over those years where what was said or done by interviewers or me during my interviewing session could foretell to anyone, including myself, what my future job successes and failures would be. I did what, according to the U.S. Bureau of Labor Statistics, approximately five million persons will do on many occasions each year in the United States: seek employment. Like so many others, I have had the good fortune of getting employment from time to time based on an interviewer's acceptance. Looking back, I find it interesting that I received more rejections than offers for employment after being interviewed.

What made the difference on those fewer occasions when I was successful, considering that I was always myself? Maybe most of the time other applicants had simply been better qualified than I was. "Sure, that's the most plausible explanation," I thought. But one day, while I was leading a typical job interviewing session, an incident occurred. Near the conclusion of her interview, the applicant, a seemingly capable person, asked me, "What exactly am I expected to say? Why should you hire me over someone else, given that I know that I am qualified for this job? What's going to mark the critical difference in your mind between me and other applicants?" This wasn't the first interview I had conducted. Anxiously, I began shuffling my page of questions and the notes I had taken. Quickly, I glanced over her application and resume again for the umpteenth time, then replied, "I'm sorry, but I'm not sure yet. Perhaps someone else may be better qualified?" She then asked incredulously, "As an interviewee or prospective employee?" Later, I was struck by the uncomfortable realization that what I was practicing was mostly meaningless. In other words, what she politely meant was, "I came here looking for an employment opportunity, and what you have subjected me to is nonsense!"

Unfortunately, a good job interview performance frequently reflects nothing more than a dubious portrayal of social conformity. At the time of this publication, over 350 books were currently available about job interviewing for job-seekers and organizations, reinforcing that cloudy vision. Unlike those, we will approach job interviewing as an organizational activity that is not disconnected or isolated from the organization, the applicant, and the future work to be performed. Participants, preparations, methodologies, session conditions, future work environments, and what's intended are factors requiring careful consideration before and during the interview. Human Performance Technology (HPT), a more recent academic discipline, is used in this work's development. HPT relies on interdisciplinary studies and practical applications in diagnosing the causes of human performance gaps in organizational settings. Then suitable interventions are offered to eliminate or narrow such gaps. A better means of managing the job interview as a decision-making business process is the intent here. The employee selection process requires standards and the same scrutiny that would be applied to account procedures, quality control appraisals, customer services, and other business activities, because like them, it is also an integral part of achieving successful and profitable business outcomes. Unlike shooting craps, when hiring, every employer can determine to a formidable extent the final position of the dice before they are cast.

The unique nature and characteristics of employment and individuals generally must be given ample consideration, because connecting these two subjects is why the interview exists. In 2004, job interviewing principles and practices still relied heavily on twentieth-century assumptions and techniques. Nowadays, shown too often, as being unfair, unreasonable, impractical, contradictory and ineffective for contemporary employment goals. This means that a new approach in job interviewing, as presented and developed here, must better serve the interview's dual purposes, more deliberately fulfilling an employer's and a job seeker's mutual business concerns through a new "best" practice.

We begin by looking at U.S. employment generally, its common business characteristics and interactions, because it serves two significantly distinct purposes. Important distinctions of employment are illustrated that separate personal and business concerns. Interviewer conduct and support strategies are presented. Employment interviewing should be conducted as business because that is the only certain framework common to both applicant and interviewer.

Next, individuals and applicants are considered. Concepts relating to personal achievement, critical thinking, intelligence, capability, motivation, readiness, interest, and intent are explored. Clarifying those ideas for the reader and bringing a fuller appreciation of how customary nuances in job interviewing can affect their recognition and expression.

Finally, a new, seamless interviewing approach and methodology is introduced. As in other business activities, various tasks can be tracked and flow more effectively if the causality of linked factors is carefully delineated, intertwining the employer and applicant together in a mutually comprehensive business encounter that enhances best efforts and diminishes reliance on more personal or social inclinations. Here, an employer and an individual are shown how to consider aspects of a future business arrangement through a realistically objective focus.

Interview practitioners will find this book a welcome job aid, providing a solid conceptual foundation and a practical methodology for conducting sensible and meaningful job interviews. Individuals, who have suffered through job interviews, befuddled and bristling underneath because of those inane questions and comments directed at them, will find comfort and greater strength if faced with similar encounters in the future. First-time job-seekers will become aware of broader issues that could affect their selection and job choices, leading them to more thoughtful and constructive approaches for landing the positions they desire. Managers of personnel should find invaluable tips for increasing and maintaining their pool of competent and productive employees. Internal business relations are aligned with studies in personality and social behavioral dynamics rather than that static presumptiveness—"One size fits all." Such an alignment provides useful insights on how personal bias and misunderstandings in business relationships develop into major employment concerns.

This book does not contain advice or directions on how to recruit applicants, prepare cover letters and resumes, or perform job searches. First, its design and purpose is to cause a critical rethinking of the interview's purpose. Showing how its essential business premise may be undermined by common but inappropriate session conditions and expectations: those employment notions that most managers and their employees or applicants consider often, but rarely can comfortably discuss with one another. Such ideas are based on personal beliefs, having no merit of purpose in business other than the questionable sharing of someone else's self-centered feelings. "Power governing rights" in work relations often act as a counterproductive force, causing practical business intents to be confused with personal motives that are inconsistent with business objectivity and merit. A new, connective approach to employment interviewing will be designed step by step, prescribing a means for keeping the interview purpose on the business of doing future business for those on both sides of the table. Throughout these pages, your thinking will be provoked. Upon completion, employers, interviewers and applicants will have more to seriously consider and constructively act upon in improving the business quality of the employment interview.

In this book, any expressed or implied names of persons and organizations written are used for illustrative purposes only and such inclusion or association in the context of events or situations posed is not a statement of fact or evidence of an actual occurrence.

Introduction

Despite volumes of critical research devoted to the job interview and its related issues over a span of eighty years, little has changed in the way job interviews are conducted. Yet, globalization, free market theory, rapid innovation, information knowledge and technology, total quality management, continual improvement, employee diversity, cross-training, quick adaptation, evolving work force, urban sprawl, and so forth embody today's U.S. business realities. Job interviews should be constructed, presented, and evaluated not only to select the best applicant for this new business world, but also as a means of standardizing this critical business process so that it can be more objectively reviewed and improved upon by organizations.

Are most employment interviews, as commonly conducted, nonsense? Do interviewers favor applicants who are better at job interviewing more so than those who aren't? Understandably, interviewers would prefer a situation that makes them feel at ease. Applicants who are better at job interviewing would also be better at promoting that feeling. In most interviews, the two are strangers, sharing the interviewer's space. Without doubt, this arrangement gives an advantage to those applicants who interview better. If this distinction marks the important difference between those who get a job offer and those who don't, then organizations should prefer applicants who do a better job of interviewing. Applicants obviously are not in position to do any other performance for the organization, since they haven't been hired yet. This would mean that those applicants who typically interview poorly would more than likely continue to do poorly after being hired. Strongly indicating that the prospective employer's business interest is best served by hiring those applicants who have demonstrated the most outstanding interview performances—although once they are hired, that is not the job the employer will be paying them to do.

Well-known job interviewing practices pose a contradiction of purpose: hire the best interviewee or the best-qualified applicant for the job? Most employment interviews as commonly conducted prior to this book are orientated towards personal favoritism rather than a business proposition. Employers, their interview representatives, and applicants would all be better served by conducting such encounters in keeping with their respective and mutual business interests only. That the well-worn job interview has, unfortunately, served primarily a social rather than a business function for too long will be made evident.

The job interview is an employer's business process for evaluating and selecting individuals who are expected to fulfill an employer's work objectives. It is not a job performance for those who are seeking to be employed. Applicants are not yet employees, and they are not paid to perform job interviews. Employer representatives are paid for this job performance. These distinctions are not trivial; they significantly influence the direction, quality, and perceptions of interviewer and applicant thinking, as well as their observable behaviors, ultimately concluding in gains and losses to the organization or someone.

Informational exchange during the interview is not an idealized social interaction or a casual happenstance conducted for the sake of getting to know someone. It's a pragmatic business encounter for evaluating and then making the best business deal. Do businesses serve customers for the potential of realizing a gain or for the purpose of rewarding privilege? Is it prudent for customers to purchase goods and services blindly? In trade, an exchange without a reasonable perception of worth by either is simply not a business proposition. Job interviewing is trade. Yet, here are just a few of the commonly held assumptions and beliefs on the part of managers, interviewers, employees, and applicants that will be examined, which belie that fundamental fact:

- A company's workers are like family.
- Businesses compete against each other.
- Critical thinking and common sense are basically the same.
- Past work performance must indicate ability more than circumstance.
- "Organizational fit" is a sensible employer motive.
- A person must have the necessary abilities to judge another's fitness for particular employment, or they wouldn't have been given that responsibility.
- To be employed is a privilege or entitlement.
- Employment is a need.
- Interviewer's questions should require quick and definite answers.

Job interviewing has been and is the most neglected and irrational business activity in U.S. organizational practice today. Many consider employment as merely a social act of affiliation. It is not. It is a unique arrangement for achieving some economic usefulness. Yet for centuries, some employers and those employed have viewed their working relationship from different levels. Those employers who were economically secure seldom identified organizational employment of others as purely an economic premise. Instead, they tended to recognize such arrangements as a means of obtaining some lofty personal aspirations while indulging a social benefit: "Let them eat cake." Meanwhile, employees recognized the same arrangement as a means of obtaining personal economic benefits because of economic needs and desires: "Where's the beef?" Today, looking down or up, mutual business utility, and not provincial ideologies, is what makes this relationship most productive and useful.

Even today, employers and employees struggle to maintain a comfortable balance between what's voluntary and obligatory from those old, yet persistent, employment perspectives. So that each can maintain and achieve those things desired and needed. Often we become confused, taking for granted another's motivation and interest, as though they were in some way bound to our own personal perceptions and values. We then take leaps, expecting that others should follow. Instead, tensions and misunderstandings are created from our own delusions. It will be shown that job interviewing today must be based more on rational business concerns than on personal ones and how conveniently the latter, given the best intentions, can overshadow the former. Most importantly, changes in practices can be easily established and executed by employers that applicants can follow, thus overall limiting the entry of those intrusions of a personal nature, which more correctly belong outside the business relationship.

Current U.S. hiring philosophy can trace its origins to Old World customs of class nobility. Generations to date have persisted in following a more refined but similar job placement practice based on personage that is no longer suited to contemporary business conditions. In the past, a noble bestowed the privilege of protection and favor upon whomever he or she liked, and in return the beholden pledged allegiance and was allowed to eke out a living as part of the lord's realm. The lord or company controlled tangible things in the environment. Whether it was brawn or other needed resources, it could be identified clearly upon the landscape and possibly secured. Strength of the principal's success depended on the control and manipulation of obvious power and dumb luck.

Do job applicants offer themselves or their abilities for sale to prospective employers? Like the produce in a market; most will be subject to an examination for blemishes and firmness, so that another individual previously "picked" may find them pleasingly wholesome. Sadly, the business organization regards and encourages this cursory appraisal as meaningful, but typically is unable to explain how or substantiate why that is so. To those applicants who believe they are for sale, it is an understandable mistake. As mentioned, we—meaning employers, employees, interviewers, and applicants—have tended to see the job interview as our parents and grandparents did: sell yourself, or make a good impression on the selecting official, and you may be chosen. "This house has a lot of character; when can we see inside?" asked the couple looking at pictures of houses for sale. "Well, I will be happy to show it to you, but don't be disappointed. It's been completely gutted inside and is not at all functional," remarked the realtor. Metaphors are convenient expressions that can help us to understand something by comparisons, but individuals are not static propositions. We have the internal property of self-actualization. We are able to offer what we think and know we possess at moments in time only. Persons can only sell abilities because most of what we are is speculative and evolving.

"Educated," "wealthy," "personable," "powerful," "intelligent," "talented," and the like, as well as their opposites, are like badges. Unconsciously, we wear them with pride or uncertainty, attempting dubious recognition by others of our hidden value to do that which we can do for them and ourselves. "Bum," "graduate," "laborer," "teacher," "politician," "businessperson," etc.—from afar, dissimilar objects can appear indistinguishable, and with nearness, only parts of a particular object may be apparent to the sight. Seeing to little of importance or seeing much that is irrelevant in a job interview makes sound business choices more careless than calculating. Making a good impression—on what basis? Informational and adaptive abilities have become more significant than merely employing warm bodies with each succeeding generation. During the interview, these important qualities in applicants can remain hidden because of commonly accepted protocols and both participants' conduct. As for luck, it's still around, but now it is sought after in the business world through the pursuit of innovation.

Our private economic futures will be more occasioned by a pattern of uncertain economic probabilities. Like the family farm, patriotism by businesses and employee longevity will become rarer conditions within the United States and elsewhere. Also, each succeeding generation becomes more dependent on commercial enterprises to fulfill needs and desires. Economic dislocation for individuals and businesses will occur more frequently than in the past. Commercialization needs adequate consumption and profitability to sustain and expand itself. It is not a naturally occurring phenomenon, but rather a deliberate human industry for buying and selling. Paradoxically, employment as means of obtaining our needs and desires advances consumption while also inhibiting an enterprise's profitability, being that employment has been the major expense item to organizations. Communicative and production technologies, discriminatory wholesale pricing structures, inter-nation alliances, credit/debt expansion, and other human manipulations give advantages to those commercial enterprises with the most financial leverage. Certainly, given these conditions, whereby cash is king and a resourceful market protector, higher production at lower labor cost will continue advancing a vexing employment reality for organizations and the public at large. For job applicants and employers alike, three perspectives will increasingly influence employment relationships in the future:

Informational Literacy
Employment Instability
Job Performance

Informational literacy means the ability to interpret, comprehend, communicate, and utilize specific information in particular situations. What's understood as intended can lead to wasteful actions and questionable results, whether machinery, devices, paper, or persons are conveying symbols or words. The ability to properly deliver, receive, and process information in conducting personal and commercial business will continue to grow in importance. Job interviewing is simply informational business exchange to exact an economic agreement. But as will be shown, too often, this exchange is distorted and made difficult due to foolish expectations and non-business motives: an appraisal of the perceived natures of the buyer or seller. Instead of what's for sale, its overall value to each, and the conditions of exchange.

Employment instability will make personal economic benefits harder to maintain for more individuals. Niche businesses historically bound to communities are generally bailing out, relocating, and going bankrupt at ever-accelerating rates because their goods and services must compete in local markets with larger regional, national, and international enterprises that can more easily reduce operating expenses faster while maintaining profitability longer. As smaller businesses are squeezed, so also are new businesses finding it more difficult to establish themselves in local markets. Larger numbers of individuals will earn less in compensation per living cost, will commute further to work, will depend more on bargain shopping, will work longer hours, and will have longer and higher debt obligations. The U.S. labor market grows larger while the demand for domestic labor shrinks, making a quality living standard through employment more difficult for organizations to give and for individuals to obtain.

Since employers do the hiring, they should know for what reasons a worker is needed. Job-seekers that have a reasonable expectation of what may be needed from them will be better able to connect with specific employer needs. The fulfillment of job needs has become a more realistic proposition than employment longevity for both.

That employees' work for themselves and not their employers is not new. It is a business agreement between the two for accomplishing employer objectives, having three aspects: adaptability, efficiency, and quality. These conditions can also be defined and measured for any business process and anticipated to varying degrees. Job performance as evaluated by employers is the modern business condition and not a worker's employment status. Employers do not hire individuals because they want employees, and individuals do not employ themselves because they want employers. Delivering particular mental efforts will become more important as the twenty-first century advances. Technology has enabled a single worker to do more distinct tasks in less time, which means they have more job-related mental considerations per time. A job-seeker's best option for continued and broader entry opportunities is to have the highest adaptability, efficiency, and quality of actions in accomplishing an employer's work objectives.

A better appreciation of the significance of the job interview can be seen through employment's other door—the exit. Being involuntarily discharged, and the associated losses caused by unemployment and the major hassle of starting over, can befall anyone. Getting a new employment offer can be particularly difficult when a previous employment separation was not on neutral or favorable terms. A prospective employer may be suspicious for the wrong reasons about hiring someone that most recently became unemployed. Evidence or trial by jury is not a consideration in proving the merit of a prospective hire's previous demise. The discharged individual may have more intense feelings of resentment also, especially if that person thinks their job performance had been appropriate and was given no hint or reason to doubt otherwise prior to dismissal. Being dismissed is an uncomfortable burden to carry and one that is difficult to explain to others wanting details. Explanations are easily misunderstood as sour grapes or disgruntled ramblings, because the listener has no factual references. Not understanding the reasoning behind a business decision that affects you adversely is bad enough, but nonetheless, it is plausible. A person may get to know someone and just not like him or her because of personal feelings. By contrast, liking or disliking an applicant on a personal level seems highly irrational as the result of a job interview.

"Tell me about yourself," the interviewer asked.

"Well, I can read and write. And I enjoy doing math," responded the applicant.

"Of course, but I want to know about you—your strengths and weaknesses. What motivates you? How do you see things?" asked the interviewer.

"Huh, for what reason? I'm not looking for a favor or a benefactor. All I want is a job so I can earn some money," replied young Einstein.

Patiently the interviewer remarked: "Well Al, I know my questions may seem odd. But it's important to know that we can have a comfortable working relationship—get along. Will you fit in? What do you see yourself doing five or ten years from now? What do you enjoy doing in your spare time—any hobbies? Relax, just be yourself and talk to me."

"I don't know. I daydream a lot about different things. Have you ever considered relativity?" responded Albert, his impatient frown changing to a curious smile.

With skepticism, the interviewer dismissed him. "Yeah, I think about them often. It's been nice talking with you, Albert. We'll consider your application and let you know something in a few weeks."

Later that same day…

Interviewer: "That young fellow Albert was one of the most arrogant and uncooperative applicants that I have interviewed in a long time. Can you imagine, he wants to work for this company, and right off the bat, he questioned me! Had the nerve to get personal with me about my family. Poor guy, he hasn't learned that negative responses foretell a disagreeable attitude in general. Too defensive, a loner; he would never be able to function well in a group. I wish him luck."

Coworker: "Oh, that's a shame. He's the boss's nephew."

Interviewer: "Yeah, with a little luck I'm sure he'll be a great team player and a wonderful asset. You think we can get him started tomorrow?"

All things considered, business decision-making by definition must be presumed to proceed rationally. Poor decisions are by choice, but not intentional. To assume otherwise would mean businesspersons desire to make poor decisions, which would obviously be an absurd notion. An employment separation for whatever reasons has a mutual history (management/employee) that may have incorrect and irrational aspects; but new employee placement carries no mutual history. Actions and judgments in interviewing are shaped and made in light of a present circumstance while looking forward, with the following conditions typically present:

- The interviewer is the decision-maker.
- The interviewer and applicant are strangers.
- What's required from one another may not have been fully presented or understood by either.
- Little time for critical thought is available to the applicant or interviewer.
- There are no interviewing standards or measures present.

With these conditions, an interviewer's personal feelings are what matter most, because there are no tangible alternatives present to base a business decision on, barring the blatant display of obnoxious behavior or offensiveness on the part of an applicant. How could an applicant be disliked on anything but a personal level? They certainly don't know each other and have no specific business reference points in common for mutual consideration. Most important, however, is the fact that it is much easier to be desirous of and adjust to a situation that makes one feel at ease. The interviewer has controlling influence in the well-known interview situation.

We see many strangers every day in our comings and goings and at times may exchange pleasantries and brief talk without the slightest uneasiness. But finding a stranger perched on the doorstep of our home would make most of us a feel a little uneasy. It is not merely a case of being offended because our personal space has been violated. Our disdain is buttressed by our own belief that the offender should have known better and is therefore guilty of insult. Interviewer opinion is primarily formed towards finding situational ease, or what's personally desirable, during the traditional interview session. Unfortunately, session objectivity for all is lost when this natural human tendency is left unguarded, because the interviewer and applicant have incorrectly focused their concerns. Whom an interviewer takes a liking to may have little to do with the real or mutual purpose that brought these strangers together in the first place, leaving a possible job connection stymied by shadowy notions and unwarranted personal assumptions without business validity. Business organizations are nobody's home, despite feelings to the contrary. In one instance, a person works to earn, and in the other, he or she works without compensation.

Employee hiring decisions, from the standpoint of those that have interviewed job applicants, would no doubt be viewed as the careful result of some meaningful exercise. If pressed, however, they would probably admit that applicant selection is a crapshoot! "Try to hire the best and hope for the best." Given qualified candidates for a particular position, the one who gets the job is the one they enjoyed interviewing the most—"I liked him/her." If you were traveling by bus across country, and you wanted some enjoyable conversation along the way, you would probably invite a talk show host rather than a mathematician to tag along. Moreover, that old saying, "It's not what you know, but who you know, that counts" seems as true today as in years past.

When asked what performance criteria his recruiters and interviewers used in judging applicants, a vice president of human resources remarked, "Well, selecting an applicant is mostly a subjective matter. After all, it takes considerable experience to develop the ability to properly read an individual. Unlike in sales, my staff does not produce results—employees or jobs. They just try to make a meaningful assessment of a ready-made package and hire the best available. They learn to know what the job calls for, and how to probe for hidden meanings in an applicant's responses. We look for positive work indicators like alertness, intelligence, ability, personality, enthusiasm, experience, and cooperation. We don't only want good workers, but good citizens of the corporation as well. Finally, interviewers match the best candidate to the job. As a rule, we give our newer staff ample opportunities to screen applicants. Over time, they develop better discernment and comfort in evaluating various types of individuals. Like I said, it takes considerable experience."

Acquiring the ability to read an individual is truly an amazing feat. Suppose the Messiah popped up in downtown New York; should he appear clean-shaven and in a business suit? "Gosh, I misread him. I thought he was just another vagrant. Please oh please, give me a chance to make amends." By what means do recruiters learn and remember the content, knowledge, and abilities required for various jobs? Those, they may have little or no experience with. How exactly do they identify positive work indicators, and for what reasons? Is past employment history a good indicator of capability, ability, or past circumstances? Should corporate employees owe some special allegiance or citizenship to a corporation? Finally, on what criteria are his interviewers measured to determine their competence in assessing various types of individuals? Considerable experience based on faulty knowledge and practice results in, at best, mediocrity.

"Team player," "communicator," "outgoing," "hasty," "humorous," and "indifferent" are all personality traits. "Individualistic," "quiet," "solitary," "deliberate," "serious," and "curious" are also personality traits. Given candidates with these variable traits, who should be chosen to do work for the organization? Why does the absurdity of divining others' personalities and a perceived affinity with strangers remain of such paramount importance in the applicant selection procedure? Is the job interview more about assessing presumed motives than predicting work capabilities? From the organization's perspective, what should the specific purpose of the interview be? Certainly, no applicant can read an interviewer's mind, and vice versa.

Are traditional job interviews conducted in a way to justify mutual business decision-making, or are they conducted in a way to promote personal favor? For their part, many applicants view with justifiable suspicion their impending job interviews as business irony, more akin to preparation for a dance with a blind date, where the tunes to be played are as mysterious as one's date. Some spend time rehearsing and choreographing a variety of steps in hopes of moving flawlessly through a dance routine. They wonder if it will be a slow, melodic dance of few and easy movements or fast-paced and set to quick and perhaps changing tempos? Should they or their partner lead? After the brief embraces, hand touching and solo moves, many an applicant exits the dance trying to remember the tune and, worse, wishing they had a better partner. The fact that applicants for different jobs spend time and money to prep with prepackaged interviewing materials indicates the underlying intent of the well-known interview process. Select applicants that have conducted an interview well, rather than selecting future employees that may perform well.

Far too many interviewers who are paid to shoulder the essential and primary responsibility of this business encounter erroneously assume that conducting a job interview is merely an intuitive process: a soft-fuzzy means of predicting employability rather than a means of foretelling successful work performance of a prospective hire. Of course, a kindred spirit floating about the workplace can be quaint. But interviewers who engage in flights of fancy when hiring do a disservice to themselves, to applicants, and to the organizations they represent. Fortunately, this has less to do with the interviewer and more to do with outdated procedures.

Today's job applicants are seeking a mutual business relationship through employment and not a sophisticated form of serfdom or even friendship. All applicants are vessels of potential that may lend value to an organization. Interviewers must have proper reasons for choosing as they do, and these must have transparency, so that confidence in the interviewing process itself is apparent to employers and applicants alike. Transparency raises business confidence by minimizing misrepresentations and suspicions, thus lowering the mutual risk of a poor deal for either party. It is what the payer is hiring an individual to accomplish, and not what the interviewer or applicant may want, that is paramount. Are the interviewer and applicant able to mutually see and understand what has to be done? Can a more credible assessment of an applicant's future worth to the organization be undertaken? Shouldn't the interview session facilitate finding answers to those questions? Overcoming outdated perspectives and common interviewing mistakes should not be difficult for the interviewer and applicant, given a new and practical alternative based on a clear understanding of what's mutually important.

During the time this book was being written and researched, television began introducing various reality-based game shows. One such show that garnered high viewer support and ratings dealt with hiring one individual among several pre-screened candidates. The chosen contestants competed in simulated business games. Then judges, competitors, and the television audience openly reviewed and evaluated contestants' performances in terms of demonstrated business savvy. Yet, the opportunity of employment is not a contest between applicants and drawn-out affairs by employers for the sake of TV ratings. The philosophy behind and the reasons for seeking employment are serious matters for individuals and businesses. For instance, an employer is paying a college-educated person to do certain work, when that worker is unable to read and write at a necessary twelfth-grade level, is a scandalous situation in the twenty-first century. A poor-quality living standard due to unemployment or inadequate income, causing personal material losses, emotional stress, and hardship to persons and their families, is also a sober matter.

1
Why Employment?

Two farmers met in town one afternoon. One farmer complained that he was falling behind schedule getting his field plowed. The other farmer irritably remarked to the complaining farmer, "I don't see how you put up with that. When work's got to be done, it's got to be done. Harry can't cut it no more." "Yeah," replied the troubled farmer, "but Harry's been solid and reliable for many years." The other farmer answered, "Sure. But it isn't like y'all really know one another. How many times has he sat down to dinner with you? Put him to pasture and get a new mule."

Somewhere in the not-too-distant past, some paternal or maternal, well-meaning business souls derived the notion that employees wanted to be adopted into an extended family—the company. This surrogate family would imbue the employee with a sense of purpose, a sense of togetherness, shared values, common expectations, and shelter in stormy weather. You may recall a similar situation known as primary schooling. In that scenario, children went to a place with a lot of other kids they didn't know, and only a select few were ever invited to a child's family dinner.

Employment's Purpose

Adult workers must share common space and work together towards common organizational aims, but they enjoy one another by choice. Since employment and business are both subject to legal rights, such practices have been defined in part according to *Black's Law Dictionary* as follows: "Employment is a voluntary agreement whereby a worker is directed and controlled by others as to the means, details, and what is to be accomplished from his or her work activity in exchange for consideration(s). *Business is employment*, occupation, profession, or commercial activity engaged in for gain or livelihood" (Black 1979, italics added). Employment serves two distinct purposes:

- Fulfillment of an employer's need(s) based on manifest and finite business expectations.

- Fulfillment of an individual's need(s) based on personally variable expectations.

If an employee's activities and work environment provide other desirable aspects to him or her, they have derived a bonus distinct from the intended legal purpose of hire. It is a slippery proposition in the larger scheme of things as to whether an employee likes related parts of or their entire employment situation. "The outcome of a person's decision to remain in or leave his job is dependent on the relative strength of the forces to remain and to leave" (Vroom 1964, 330). It is quite reasonable that they may hate their jobs but love the pay! Also, some job applicants may be more focused on getting employment than doing a job. Since job service is what an employer is paying for, an individual's employment preferences are not the employer's first concern. Applicants who want or need particular employment considerations, such as persons with disabilities, have a right to ask for them, but employers also have the right of reasonable refusal in obliging such request. Applicants' needs are personally variable, but job vacancies exist because organizational human resource needs are unfulfilled.

Individuals seek employment primarily for personal economic benefit, or to have access to personal resources. The engineer may seek employment with an aeronautical firm to build that modern airplane, or the commentator/reporter may become employed by media to have an audience for his or her personal work. Plane assembly in the backyard and mounting a loudspeaker on one's roof simply wouldn't provide enough for those individuals. In every employment case, it is a personal, economic motive and not a drive for social affiliation that is the job-seeking imperative. With employers, to what degree will focusing on sociability and personal preferences be more a risk than a benefit in maintaining a business's functional integrity and quality output? For instance, should participation or failure to participate in the office party, or company picnic, or to work beyond a personally preferred time, be an indication of some positive or negative feelings that can accentuate or diminish work performance? Mullen and Copper (1994) concluded that efforts to increase productivity by pumping up group pride are not likely to be effective. Employment considerations of a non-economic nature can be more distracting and burdensome than helpful to the organization and its employees. Philosophies carried by interviewers and applicants of a more social rather than business character send confusing messages that can undermine the business purpose of the job interview.

Do not all workers within an organization want what's best for the organization? Do not all members within a family want what's best for the family? Maybe in *Pleasantville,* a movie which spoofed 1950's television lifestyles, this was always true; but real-life family members then and now can be alienated due to differing expectations. Yet, in spite of differing personal objectives, persons can and do function well together. Unlike organizational employees, family members are not by choice forever a family group.

Employment does not mean joining an organization; it means working for an organization. It is not a social act for voluntary participation or for seeking some desirable group affiliation. It is a business arrangement for personal gain. Bill Gates, the founder of Microsoft, at one time was reported to be one of the richest men in the world. He also worked as principal owner, and not an employee, which meant he determined the extent of his personal business obligations to his organization. Choosing to conduct business meetings in his pajamas may raise some eyebrows, but not much more. Those who get paid the big bucks are always deserving, whether they do any work or not, because somebody is willing to pay—that's business.

A couple went to New York for vacation. As part of their visit, they planned to purchase a diamond ring. The husband, who had intended to purchase this ring for his wife, was prepared and related the following story. They went into the diamond district to shop and found a ring that his wife wanted. It had a price tag of five thousand dollars. First, wanting to appear competent to the merchant, the husband used a loupe to examine the diamond. Then he reached into his suit jacket pocket and pulled out a wad of twenty-five crisp one-hundred-dollar bills. He counted and carefully arranged the bills in neat stacks on the counter in front of the merchant. "My wife and I will return home to Michigan tomorrow. Here is twenty-five hundred dollars cash for that ring. Do we have a deal?" "Have a nice trip," replied the merchant. The customer slowly began picking up each bill, while telling the merchant, "I don't know what your profit margin is on this ring. But we both know that if you don't accept my offer you would not lose twenty-five hundred dollars, but only some of your potential profit. Do you think that other merchants will pass on a similar offer? Do you really want to wait until this afternoon, tomorrow, or maybe months from now to gain a certain potential profit on this single ring, when you could be assured a smaller profit right now?" "Three thousand dollars cash,' said the merchant. The ring was purchased for $2,730.

Those who get paid the big bucks are able to do so for three reasons: being in the right position, having an opportunity, and a readiness to take the advantage. Being in the right position allows them to be where that type of money can be had. Opportunity is the realization that something big can be gained now. A readiness to take an advantage means seizing upon the opportunity but has nothing to do with future work or effort. Some business executives, entertainers, and athletes are prime examples. For them to function successfully will require, on their part, effort and work to continually produce. But that comes after the fact. Any person who believes that ability, hard work, and effort alone should make them extraordinary money has missed the point. Although someone's ability may be extraordinary, without positioning, opportunity, and readiness, getting access to "big money" can remain an elusive prospect. Look around and consider the talents (gold) you or others may possess. Who's buying what, and at what price, makes the big difference in earnings. One's circumstances can be arranged individually as well as altered by the unexpected, but only proper preparation can make the latter less important over time.

Economic wealth and power cannot be self-made. It is acquired from someone or something. In the beginning, the American Indians were more powerful and wealthy economically than the European settlers were. Yet, the Indians accepted mere trinkets in exchange for valuable property, because ownership for wealth accumulation had no meaning for them. The Indians held no position relative to a European standard. Indians saw trade and not wealth development as a big opportunity. Finally, they were not ready, because they were unprepared to deal with unexpected circumstances. On the other hand, the settlers and the government prepared and planned in order to create unique opportunities for themselves.

Employment, ownership, big earnings, transactional values, positioning, opportunity, and readiness are independent of each other. Attending a prestigious college is a prime example of the interplay between such factors. Such enrollment will not provide a particular character or intellectual advantage to an individual, but such an environment offers an optimal condition for developing unique associations and knowledge. Such positioning can significantly improve one's chances for more exclusive economic gains in the future. Understanding employment for employment's sake is paramount to understanding an organization's employment interviewing purpose. Prestige, power, wealth, ambition, and so forth are unique topics with different dynamics. Employment is simply an obligation we all may need to carry to achieve some personal reward(s).

Organizational Commitment and Dedication

John is a forty-two-year-old crew foreman for a large landscaping firm. He never completed high school and has worked for the same company for twelve years. Mike is a twenty-one year old college student who works as a laborer for the same firm during his summer school break. Mike hopes to one day be a botanist. David is also a laborer for the landscaping company, and is the same age as Mike. David earnestly wants different employment and has no specific career ambitions. Which of the three is most committed or dedicated to their employer, and why? Each of them does a good job.

A broad concept of organizational commitment refers to the extent to which a worker identifies with and is involved in an organization (Porter et al., 1974). This notion is untenable, given the legal definition of employment. It is suggested that organizations do the following if convinced that such a concept is worth pursuing: in lieu of the company picnic, party, and/or retreat, buy lottery tickets often and distribute them to all those workers who would normally be expected to attend such affairs. Be forewarned, though: there could be a big winner. The big winner could be your best employee, and he or she may feel obliged to change commitments abruptly. This should not suggest that a worker's personal motivation to work does not extend further than their economic need, but rather that employment is an arrangement for fulfilling economic needs and is not a need itself.

Most paid workers do not have as their primary concern the organization's welfare, but rather their own quality of life. This is a mature, practical, and sensible philosophy. Glew et al. (1995), in a study on employee participation, found that if an organization's purpose were to exploit workers' creative abilities in solving work problems without sharing the profits that come from the use of their ideas, the participation program would fail. Quality of life goes way beyond an individual's "bread and butter concerns"; it is the sum total of being, feeling, thinking, and relating to the environment of self and all that is one's life. Obviously, for most, employment will play a large part in fulfilling our particular quality of life concerns. Any worker who truly understands this offers a silent but implicit business agreement to protect the organization's interest, and thereby their own.

Does an assembly line worker at Ford really care what logo hangs on her back? Couldn't General Motors provide the same employment benefits? Commitment and loyalty are cute slogans, but at the end of the day, what counts is the employee's or the organization's successes. Employers who think they can identify organizational commitment and dedication in their employees are deceiving themselves. Another's level of commitment and dedication may belie sincerity, and one may never really know another's heartfelt yearnings. Logically, John would probably have more employee dependency than the other two workers would, because he has more reasons to stay. But a belief that John's work behavior is an indication of commitment or dedication to his employer holds no weight. In business, to be motivated towards one's best self-interest is more than enough as long as manifest employment intents are being met. Good job performance is value for any organization, with or without pronouncements of true personal motives and feelings on the part of employees, no matter whether management thinks otherwise.

Thought Conformity

High-performance organizations take a definite approach to achieve ever-increasing levels of quality, profitability, and customer satisfaction through work performance interventions. In terms of hiring, however, employers—even those with high performance initiatives—typically fall short in interviewing for new hires. It is often assumed that some quasi-feeling of sameness in perspectives and a perceived sociability during the interview are integral ingredients for success in the workplace. Organizations have perceived the abstraction "organizational fit" as though it was a prerequisite for deriving favorable singular or collective work outcomes. Cooperating in a working relationship to achieve objectives and goals is not some "new era" thinking. It is as old as humanity. Conformity with protocols, standards, and regulations can be a positive thing in that it can allow frequent processes to have consistency, enabling better control over time. Yet, it can suppress creativity and objective thinking through the denial of individual expression (Cialdini 1993). In an earlier report, it has been suggested that higher-quality solutions to certain problems are obtained when group members have substantially different perspectives and these differences are expressed and used in arriving at decisions (Hoffman and Maier 1961). Effective personnel management is a business application to derive acceptable work outcomes. It is not a tool for creating conformity in personal beliefs, values, and attitudes.

> In many types of cohesive groups, just as in the industrial work groups described by other investigators, *members tend to evolve informal objectives to preserve friendly intragroup relations, and this becomes part of the hidden agenda*.... Groupthink refers to a deterioration of mental efficiency, reality testing, and moral judgment that results from in-group pressures.... The more amiability and esprit de corps between individuals, the higher the probability for "groupthink," a powerful source of defective judgment. The advantages of having decisions made by groups are often lost because [of] psychological pressures that arise when members work closely together, share the same values, and above all, face a crisis situation that generates a strong need for affiliation. In these circumstances, as conformity pressures begin to dominate, "groupthink" and the attendant deterioration of decision-making set in. (Janis 1972, 8-13, italics added)

McKelvey (1969) found that organizations tend to reward employees who follow the organizational norms rather than rewarding divergent thinkers. At each promotional level, there is a selection bias toward sameness. Thus, the closer they get to the top, the more likely the management is to display mutual agreement. The suppression of contradictory information is a common strategy in "groupthink" as well as one's personal assertion of "I believe." As will be shown later, successful critical thinking, unlike so-called "common sense," requires considerations of a broader scope, and most individuals have difficulty in this regard. If those with power status are superficial thinkers, it stands to reason that persons who think critically can pose difficulty for them. Since governing power, in contrast to pure salesmanship, by definition promotes the self-delusion of having that ability to influence others towards some acceptance, those more mentally challenged but powerful are not anxious to recognize questioning minds within their circle of direct influence. Preventing contradictory thought makes their work effort (thinking) easier and self-image seem more secure.

Triandis (1996) mentions two aspects that this writer believes U.S. decision-makers must be attentive to when relating to employees and applicants. Members of individualist cultures place more value on an individual's preferences and attitudes than to group norms as explanations of behavior. Secondly, such members focus on a perception of the benefits compared to the cost in maintaining a relationship. A harmonious group is a lesser concern than individual goals and wishes. Suggesting further, such members would be more inclined to give lip service to a theme by dominant others in order to advance more important personal motives.

It seems perverse, in a nation considered the most culturally diverse and individualistic in the world, that any U.S. employer would want to advance a collectivist agenda for their workers. It is a futile proposition as long as individual lifestyles of wealth and material splendor are promoted as the ideal goals to embrace. A desire for high material consumption and greater self-reliance is a commonly-shared theme of rich and poor as well as the employed and unemployed. It is not the organization or management that one desires conformity with, but rather one's self-interest. Those with decision-making authority who are not careful may jeopardize better business outcomes through their tacit reliance on disingenuous but necessary deference to their titles. The United States emphasizes individualism, and not collectivism as in Japan (Campbell et. al. 1996; de Rivera 1989; Kashima et. al. 1995; Triandis 1996). This philosophy has and probably will continue to shape and condition U.S. citizens' temperaments, priorities, and expectations. Hui, Yee, and Eastman (1995) studied fourteen different countries and found that the more collectivist a nation was, the more satisfied were the employees with their interpersonal work relationships. Any culture can adapt any business activity readily, because business is nothing more than a transaction to accomplish something tangible. Culture, on the other hand, requires both personal and social recognition and acceptance of certain beliefs and values to exist. The hippie movement of the 1960's was an international cultural affair, but no one had to be or act like a hippie to engage in the business opportunities that that presented.

Personality Judgments

Although the desire for a comfortable relationship is normal on both sides of the hiring desk, it is the interviewer's job to represent what is in the best interest of the employer. Interviewers shouldn't try to perceive or predict personality traits of applicants. They typically lack the educational training in such matters, and interviews usually last about sixty minutes. Discerning or realizing actual personality traits with any degree of validity or reliability is therefore a dubious undertaking.

Written psychometric testing of personality traits, as a means of objectively measuring an applicant's suitability, are becoming a popular tool again with some organizations. Clinically, and in the hands of a skilled psychologist, the results on a series or battery of such tests over time are privately assessed, and then discussions take place with the test-taker. This enables the trained psychologist to elicit from the test-taker a truer assessment of that individual. No competent psychologist would ever base an evaluation of personality on mere test results without personal interface, because too many variables are present that can affect responses. There exists no proven scientific test or methodology to predict what an individual's overall personality is and, more critically, how personality trait characterizations may impact the interplay of individual traits and work behaviors. Researchers have defined over fifty pairs of traits, and to what degree someone is aggressive or passive, for example, is ill defined. Organizations would probably find astrology to be as useful an exercise as personality profiling. With only twelve zodiac houses for possible matches, it could be an easier way of defining something. A more damning indictment against personality testing has been based on moral and ethical grounds.

> Although few in the corporate ranks will ever find themselves tested in courts of law, millions have seen their lives altered with the nonscience [sic] of personality testing without even a presumption of individual guilt. The moral implications of personality testing lie not only in its inaccuracy (which, by analogy, would mean filling our jails with the innocent) but its approach to group statistical guilt. A man is accused and convicted not for any unsocial [sic] act or behavior, but for his variance, either from a norm or a projective tester's highly imaginative criteria…. The importance of impartiality of judgment is another caisson in the framework of our morality, and the partiality of much in personality testing has been questioned. (Gross 1962, 277-278)

Behavior, however, can change, and individuals are adaptable. That is one reason why persons naturally mature, and some seek professional therapy. Those that are unfamiliar with psychology often confuse personality and behavior. A clinical psychologist related the following.

A client in her middle thirties came to see me because she was having difficulty in her marriage. She was a highly successful salesperson, and during our fourth session, we exchanged the following dialogue.

> Client: I guess everything will work out okay. I mean, I love him and everything. But if it (the marriage) doesn't survive, I am sure I can rebound. I'm a trooper.
>
> Therapist: How so?
>
> Client: Well, look at my life. I am successful in my own right. I mean, I know lots and lots of people in the community. I've built my success on my ability to connect, social functions, civic affairs—I mean, I have quite a network. After all, I know being an extrovert gives me some advantage when it comes to depression and stuff like that.
>
> Therapist: You believe you're an extrovert?
>
> Client: Well, yes. Haven't you been listening? Isn't it obvious?
>
> Therapist: (Looking at notes) What is it again that you do, when you are not working or networking?
>
> Client: I put my answering machine on and relax. I really do enjoy my space whenever I can.

This client is a classic introvert in terms of personality trait dominance. However, being such has little to do with one's ability to behave in an outgoing, gregarious, or social manner. On the contrary, an introvert can display the same behavioral characteristics as an extrovert. From a clinical standpoint, the significance between the two has more to do with the different ways of coping in response to an identical circumstance. (Contributed by L. L. McKenzie, Ph.D.)

Organizations offer training, evaluations, counseling, and other performance development interventions in order to qualify work performances and not their employees. Employment interviewing as a means of determining some ambiguous and preemptive behavioral relief is an arrogant and foolish practice. Aberrant social behaviors are typically suppressed while one is actively engaged in work, and work behaviors must be identified as they occur in the job setting.

When people do work, they take on the persona of workers. Their focus and manner are intent on work activities. This is a voluntary role change, unlike Harry the mule, who is always a mule whether harnessed or not. A person can be quiet at times and/or talkative. A person can conserve energy and rise to the occasion. A person can be selfish but cooperative with others in solving a problem. Personality usually refers to the distinctive patterns of behavior (including thinking, emotions, mannerisms, and attitudes) that characterize each individual's adaptation to situations in his or her life.

Positive changes that high-performance organizations have achieved are functions of organizational development interventions and individuals—not personalities. Sifting haphazardly through applicants in search of imagined personality types typically leaves an unexamined clump with questionable value. The fact that different interviewers can look for different personality traits is problematic. Moreover, different interpretations of, and weight given to, the same information further exacerbates the problem.

Attitudes

Expressing negativity and displaying a negative attitude are not the same. The latter is characterized in employment by a frequent unwillingness to adopt a stance or execute an action based on what is reasonable. Studies have further described attitudes as consistent patterns of thoughts, feelings, and behavioral displays directed towards some aspects of relatedness. They are one's perceptions of someone else's thoughts, feelings, and behavior. Attitudes are not observed; they are inferred from behavior and expressions of emotion.

"So-and-so is arrogant, sarcastic, negative, lazy, prejudiced, not on the team, and so forth" are typically characterized as attitude problems in the workplace. Such labeling is elevated to a major bone of contention because the labeler believes that they themselves are beyond reproach or the alleged perpetrator is beyond redemption. In other words, "I didn't do or say anything wrong, so they must have a bad attitude," or "So-and-so has an attitude problem, and that's too much of a distraction to deal with." But in reality, attitude formation and expression, whether good or bad, is based on a conscious assessment, right or wrong, and not a particular circumstance. For example, a superior orders a subordinate to perform a task outside of the worker's normal routine. The worker voices an objection. "Why are you telling me?" Is the worker being difficult? Perhaps the worker has expressed difficulty or concern with the order, the expectation, the timing, the superior, others, or themselves. That persons can be disagreeable at times is not necessarily indicative of an ongoing pattern of behavior. Moods and attitudes are not the same.

Negative attitude of an employee is inferred by observing some consistent objectionable omission or commission in work behavior. Jones and Nisbett (1971, 58) suggest that "actors tend to attribute the causes of their behavior to stimuli inherent in the situation, while observers tend to attribute behavior to stable dispositions in the actor." According to these researchers, this paradox may have more to do with having more information about our own situations and more limited information about others. The real problem in this is that the observer or judge believes the attitude is stable in the actor, which leads the observer to be suspicious and distrustful of the actor, which in turn can lead to personal tension in a business relationship. The following dialogue is a good illustration of how even purely objective observations can result in problems of inference.

Boss: I don't understand them. They just don't take ownership of their work.

Manager: What do you mean?

Boss: I mean look at their reports. They're full of grammatical errors and poor expressions.

Manager: I checked the reports, and I didn't see many errors.

The boss hands a report to the manager filled with corrections and revisions.

Manager: (looking puzzled) What did you get your degree in?

Boss: A master's in English and journalism.

Manager: Did it occur to you that no one on your staff has or may ever have your writing proficiency?

Boss: I don't understand.

Manager: You believe that we should be in possession of your passion and skills for writing. Although all of us possess degrees, and some even advanced ones, to assume we should measure up to your writing standards, and then to attribute that to some unwillingness on our part, is, to say the least, unfair. If you needed carpentry work, you could hire a handyman or a licensed carpenter. Would you expect the same level of work quality from each? It is not your criticism of the report's quality that I take issue with, but that you think our failure in achieving your standard of quality was somehow deliberate on our part.

Boss: Well, if I have to do the work, what do I need you all for?

Manager: Perhaps, as a place to start? (Implying that the boss did not write the reports and it is far easier to criticize than create.)

To ascertain whether any behavioral observation during employment or the interview is indicative of an attitude problem, frustration, misunderstanding, or other area of concern. The 'judge' must ask immediately for an explanation by prefacing the request with, "When you did or said so-and-so, it made me think or feel so-and-so; is that what you meant?" What develops out of this is twofold. A situational context has been framed, and a factual reference point has been mutually evidenced. Misgivings may be rationale and mutual acknowledgment a form of redemption. Remember, attitudes are particular patterns of response, and are not isolated incidents. History is replete with those who led and those who followed, supported by acceptable attitudes of the period; only later were those collective attitudes found unreasonable at best, and at worst, contemptible.

Loyalty is defined as a faithfulness or adherence to an idea, fact, detail, conduct, or person, and is thereby the most complex and troubling attitudinal aspect within business, because it can be expressed willfully, but is unfixed. That is why the courts long ago barred the forced testimony of spouses against one another. On the other hand, trust in a business relationship is a behavioral action deriving from a mutually implicit or explicit agreement. A secretary who keeps her boss's confidences and an attorney who does his or her best to defend the guilty client are examples of behavioral trust. It is open, purposeful, and has a transactional value, whereas loyalty is more akin to fool's gold. One can claim or believe it is the stuff to trust, but only after each "working" can it be known for sure.

Morale

Business morale is a perception of a worker's "attitude" towards their job, the organization, and immediate management (Kahn and Katz 1953 616). It has also been defined as a group characteristic (Jerdee 1966), containing three components: group cohesiveness, commitment to attainment of organizational goals, and a sense of progress toward goal attainment. Whether one or both definitions are accepted, morale deemed high, low, or just right is an overreaching concept without objective value in business. The challenge in grappling with issues of morale in business is like reaching into a barrel full of snakes to pick a particular one. What is felt is a convoluted mass of ever-shifting positions in which heads or tails are hard to grasp. However, work performance in terms of activities and outcomes evidenced in both definitions, excluding organizational commitment and group cohesiveness, can be objectively isolated, appraised, and managed. Addressing the quality and/or quantity of observable facts relating to a performance and not speculating about imagined motives of workers is key (Isaac 1992). In any work group, as in any social group, the degree of cohesiveness, commitment to attainment of organizational goals, and a sense of progress toward goal attainment cannot be accurately ascertained, nor can it be manipulated on an individual basis. In contrast, individual behaviors can create observable and measurable positive or negative accomplishments.

Since morale is a particular type of attitude, it too can only be imagined or speculated about by others. We observe and consider another's action and try to find or understand what feelings, according to our limited knowledge, may have caused a person to act in a certain way. Friends, siblings, and spouses may have mixed emotions and opinions, causing rifts in relationships. Yet, a perceived trust in no further displays of questionable behavior may mend such breaches. A coworker will speak about low morale, due to workplace changes or circumstances, which leave them or others feeling uncomfortable. "I just don't think that's right," the coworker remarks. What happened due to the criminal misconduct of some priest in the U.S. Catholic Church is another example. This caused morale, or satisfaction with this organization, to deflate amongst clergy and parishioners. The fact that the church's representatives and others knew that steps would be taken to try to prevent such misconduct from reoccurring in the future will not immediately raise morale. Only time will tell to what degree morale is restored.

But this will not occur because the attitudinal states of individuals have been manipulated. Rather, the conditions within the organization change, and personal assessments in time may change. So, suppose environmental conditions don't change? Personal attitudes are personal, and the degree to which applicants and employees are able to adapt to a situation is highly variable. To see combat soldiers laughing and having a good time while on liberty in no way changes individual, emotional attitudes towards the life of war that they may routinely live with. In 2003, a newspaper article reported a national survey claiming that a majority of American workers are dissatisfied with their jobs, and the percentage of dissatisfied workers is rising. Dissatisfaction of any type is not necessarily a bad thing, because it can spark positive changes or improvement. Here, again, management and labor can create personal expectations that blur the business character of the employment arrangement, leading to emotional confusion. Maybe some employers should change conditions, or perhaps some workers need to alter their expectations or environment? The bottom line: we all want the best situation for ourselves in all respects, but employment is something we can voluntarily change; therefore, it is not a soldier's story. Do the conditions of job interviewing support its purported purpose, the interviewer, or the applicant? Getting job-pertinent information from an applicant means conditions should be neutral emotionally.

Beliefs and sentiments, like a tapestry, are woven of many threads. The business organization is like a neighborhood filled with strangers, friends, acquaintances, and potential adversaries connecting with one another as the need arises or at their pleasure. A person prospecting for a place in an organizational neighborhood may forever be a stranger to most and neither a friend nor an enemy to any. Personal expressions are interwoven into our social fabric. Whether one chooses to hang a tapestry up for common display or tuck it away until a special occasion does not diminish or accentuate its value. At will, it can be used to hide, adorn, contain, and transport many purposes. Family, personality, thought conformity, cohesion, and organizational commitment, as well as attitudes, are matters of opinion. Their interpretations can carry us in many directions. Endings that do not land within the boundary of a business zone have probably trespassed onto private, residential property. Trying to get somewhere by venturing down uncertain paths can be confusing. While reaching, the wrong place is a waste of energy and time.

2
Business Sense

A business may have legal stature, but it is devoid of consciousness, including feelings, perceptions, beliefs, values, personality, and expectations. This is a material fact. A business organization is a contrivance, apparatus, or artificial entity of selected persons drawn from society at large. Realistically, a business organization represents very narrow and definable objectives in comparison to the infinite amount of compounded informational relatedness it may employ.

Management must distinguish between, and be forever mindful of, the inherent difference between the role of a worker and that same person as a private individual. A person who quits his job or is fired would not be held to the same interpersonal scrutiny as one that quits his family or becomes divorced. The latter are considered social norms, understood in the context of rules, social conventions, and cultural standards that are currently in vogue. Organizational management must, therefore, maintain a separation between expectations of a personal flavor and those of a practical, business nature. A fuller appreciation of the complexity and fluidity of human behavior in business should be helpful in that regard. "One size does not fit all."

The Work

When organizations perceive their paid workers as beneficiaries. They taint the performance landscape by minimizing the transactional value of work. "I gave you a job. You should be grateful" is not the same as the following statement: "I needed a worker. Therefore, I hired you." The former infers a personal favor; the latter is a business reality. A worker feels their manager owes them some special acknowledgement of appreciation for doing a fine job, although that is what the worker is paid to do. The manager who assumes a subordinate's acknowledged understanding of what he or she said is the same as mutual agreement and the boss who incredulously admonishes her subordinate, "You're getting paid, aren't you?" show momentary lapses in business perspective. These types of non-business lapses are convenient and highly effective coping mechanisms used by workers. They serve to make an inability to articulate or defend one's inner reasoning or concern palatable by "saving face, not unlike an adult's reaction to a child's difficult question or incorrect behavior: "Why is the sky blue?" "Because God made it blue," replies the parent. "Why didn't He make it green?" Representing behavioral shorthand, this allows us to conclude an internally uncertain issue with quick dispatch, precluding the need to expend additional mental energy while safeguarding our inner orientations. Being right becomes more important than doing what is right. The messenger becomes more important than the message. A thought about what someone else is about becomes more significant than a business performance.

> Trying to feel what one wants, expects, or thinks one ought to feel is probably no newer than emotion itself. Conforming to or deviating from rules is also hardly new. What is new in our time is the increasingly prevalent instrumental stance toward our native capacity to play, wittingly and actively, upon a range of feelings for a private purpose and the way in which that stance is engineered and administered by large organizations... We are capable of disguising what we feel, of pretending to feel what we do not—of doing surface acting.... In surface acting, we deceive others about what we really feel, but we do not deceive ourselves. Diplomats and actors do this best, and very small children do it worst (it is part of their charm).... Another type of acting is termed deep acting, which from one point of view involves deceiving oneself as much as deceiving others.... As workers, the more seriously social engineering affects our behavior and our feelings, the more intensely we must address a new ambiguity about who is directing them (is this me or the company talking?).... In the end, it seems, we make up an idea of our "real self," an inner jewel that remains our unique possession no matter whose billboard is on our back or whose smile is on our face...This type of work effort (emotional work) calls for a coordination of mind and feeling, and it sometimes draws on a source of self that we honor as deep and integral to our individuality. (Hochschild 1983, 20-34)

Studies have shown that human behaviors have situational variance. For example, a manager may have an abrasive or impatient manner with coworkers while maintaining the highest performance ratings in customer service. To her coworkers, she is petty, demanding, argumentative, and confrontational. However, customers benefit, because this behavioral pattern is effective in minimizing and resolving complaints quickly by keeping those that directly serve customers on their toes. Whether employees perform true emotional work (defined interactions with the public) or the quasi-type, such as undefined interacting with fellow workers, they are not unlike those workers who do a non-emotional task that is either physical or mental, in that the performance becomes more a claim of the organization and less of the individual worker (Hochschild 1983). **The work done by interviewers and applicants during a traditional job interview is essentially emotional in nature and left unclaimed by the organization.**

Business Teaming

To view "teaming" as a necessity of first resort, rather than a "time and cost savings factor" or an adjunct means of accomplishing an objective, can prove inefficient and counterproductive. Interpersonal skills are practiced, social-adaptive behaviors that communicate. When someone is employed by an organization, he or she must set aside his or her own goals, at least in part, to strive for the collective goals of the organization. Worker performance must always be viewed from a business context, because management defines appropriate work performance. Yet managers obscure communication that is more effective with subordinates by creating a climate for their workers that is more conducive to military service or participation in a team sport. Perhaps this is why surveys have concluded that eighty percent of business problems stem from poor interpersonal communication. The interpersonal quality of business communication is not only how business information is exchanged and understood; it is the sense of freedom one has in being able to express it. In business, crisis events are not the norm, and the urgency of opinions can be given pause for reasoning.

>   **Supervisor:** This consultation is an attempt to clarify certain concerns that your coworkers have voiced. Although you have only been here for less than two months, they feel you are not participating in the team meetings. They would like to hear your ideas and comments concerning discussions. What are your thoughts about their concerns?
>
>   **Worker:** I'm surprised. My reading of the meetings does not provoke any special concerns or thoughts in me, and I am willing to do whatever is asked of me.
>
>   **Supervisor:** Well, we appreciate that, but we need everyone's input. Can't you be a little more forthcoming? I think you are an intelligent person, and we want to know what you think.

Worker: Sir, what I think is totally at odds with the approach taken thus far in the meetings. My mother always told me, "If you don't have anything constructive to say, don't say anything." How should I convey my thoughts when others are preoccupied with a course of action that I believe to be imprudent and ineffective? If my silence has caused this, what would my words cause? I am new here, and I am concerned about business issues and getting along. How do I do both?

This dialogue is illustrative of the paradoxical notion that aligns business relations with common social patterns of behavior. Business is a specialized arrangement to indirectly increase internal and external transactional gains. In spite of business concepts and strategies for sustaining or advancing competitive advantage through innovation, product diversity, erecting barriers, and so forth, markets drive business, and not competition. In contrast, team sports, military service, political parties, and the like do not offer products or services for sale. They arrange and develop individuals into end products (groups) for the sake of competing against other such groups. Michael Jordan, considered by many to be one of the greatest basketball players, had to alter his basketball-playing style to better accommodate team play. This resulted in championships. The work group as product exists for the sole purpose of directly winning a contested outcome. Japanese industries did not gain dominance in electronics by beating the competition. Their work groups as processing units, and not products, made and eventually sold more products, causing their competitors' market share to evaporate. A major software manufacturer does not dominate the software application market because it was victorious over competing companies. It secured a dominant market share. A sports team wins a championship because an opponent was beaten. One candidate wins the U.S. presidency because he is declared the winner in a contest. Political parties oppose each other to win legislation and maintain group member support. Self-sacrifice, loyalty, conformity, morale, compliance, and a commonality of purpose can be inherent ingredients in pursuing victory via group-applied action. It is, in essence, single-mindedness directed towards obtaining a singular outcome against a clearly defined challenge.

Oddly, authentic heroes and those deserving special recognition in the pursuit of a team goal gain legitimate distinction by not doing what's expected—the typical role. It is the breaking with team conventions, or those individual actions beyond the call of duty, which sets them apart from the group. Applicants feel victorious if the job interview results in a job offer. Interviewers win when their choices prove effective. They are not competitors, and it is no game. Nor, in reality, do applicants go head to head against one another. Contrary to glitzy advertisements, it is not a victory that business organizations covet, but rather maintenance and improvement internally as well as externally. **The job interview or business transaction was conducted successfully when and if the best person for the job according to the employer's desired knowledge, skills and abilities (KSA's) was hired for business reasons.**

Business Compliance

Within a business organization, the CEO, the investor, the receptionist, the custodian, and the salesperson are seldom on the floor at the same time or face to face with a common obstacle. Each has different personal motivations and work objectives, but more importantly, compliance towards their activities and business relationships, rather than a common viewpoint, define their purpose. From the business organization's perspective, this purpose is for work to be done in the best possible way, and if a machine can do it better, so be it. It is the work activity and results which are critical, not the worker. The field must be plowed regardless.

A Michael Jordan can be a solo player within a business organization, and the business can flourish. In fact, it is solo abilities, and not team effort, which make business organizations develop most quickly and productively. Traditional communism and socialism failed in developing successful business models because would-be high performers were handicapped by group constraints. As a work strategy, putting the ball in the hoop is a results-oriented action that can benefit the whole organization, while sharing the ball is a process-oriented action of moving the ball around with hopes of putting the ball through the net. At any given moment in business, any performer can be that competent or incompetent in getting a shot off and scoring big.

Closer to the point, unique ideas are fashioned and carried in solitary minds before others can act them upon. Mental tasks are not by analogy the same as physical tasks: "See that boulder? Let's move it by pushing all together." Sometimes it's just too heavy or awkward for members of a group to tackle. Fortunately, a single person thinks differently, decides to use a big stick, and the lever is born. The business organization that emphasizes personal learning or development for the sake of team development, rather than to derive a specific work outcome, makes an unjustified and wasteful assumption. Not all workers should or will have the same inclination and characteristics to contribute similarly on cue. Nor are those who benefit from such sponsored interventions bound to remain within the organization or improve others. The selection of what is the most appropriate "driver" in accomplishing work objectives is therefore essential. Workers from the top down are essential cogs in the organizational wheel, but they are first and always human.

Organizations must accept inevitable variability in an employee's actions as typical and reactionary. Embracing the solo player who can score versus the team player who can play the game may be the difference between mediocrity and outstanding performance at various work levels.

Employment dealings are not extensions of culture, society, or family, but merely arrangements in time established for personal gain. Again in 2002, this reality was made clear by Enron, WorldCom, and K-Mart executives to thousands of their corporate workers who lost their jobs and savings while those businesses' leaders enriched themselves. U.S. employees do have the liberty to leave employment. However, to take the liberty to rock the organizational boat—to be insubordinate or offend—does not afford societal, cultural, or family rights of continual inclusion. Compliance to authority is not an option but a requirement in employment. Feigning genuineness while buffering assaults to one's integrity can create a personal, social, and business dilemma (Collins and Brief 1995; Milgram 1974).

Misguided intents, inappropriate concerns, and questionable actions from above and below can occur often on many fronts in employment. For an employee, this trial is not over until retirement or circumstance allows one to step away from the employment turf. In the meantime, most of us can expect no early announcements, whistles, or surrender marking the end of our employment campaign. Instead, we maintain a hope that one day the choice of fulfilling needs will be more our own than those of others. **Being "on the same page" with someone during a job interview is not an acceptance of the message, but merely an acceptance of the truth of its existence.**

Business Clarity

In the Firestone Tire debacle of 2000, one of the company heads made a public apology. He took the blame for what grew into an international scandal. Although he was no doubt sincere in his apology and felt honor-bound in expressing it, had all the facts become known, he might have been exonerated from direct culpability. So how did so many defective tires get manufactured, and why did it take so long to address this problem forthrightly and publicly? Was it worker(s') error or carelessness? Did a chemical or machine process malfunction? This writer hasn't a clue. Obviously, if production were shut down to fix the problem, millions of dollars in added expenses would have been incurred. Investors may have become alarmed; personal images could have been tarnished and employees fired. Did a hopeful avoidance of financial harm to individuals or the organization forestall public disclosure? The reader might reason that maybe someone was attempting to protect the company, or perhaps company officers believed that the problem would not become so damaging. Maybe they didn't believe the problem was theirs in the first place, but rather a different company's problem. Clarifying expectations amongst workers at any job level is a major difficulty in business decision-making. With our expanding informational-relatedness, this will remain a far-too-muddled affair unless business expectations are isolated from personal ones.

Healthy business communication to derive clarity is diminished when personal expectations are elevated above business expectations. Granted, personal expectations are normal, imaginable thoughts, which are commonplace within organizations. But the expanse of information we are now inundated with is unprecedented in human history. Our new, knowledge- and information-based economy has taken root because business information has lengthened its discretionary reach. Business elitism continues to decline due to new technologies within and around organizations, making information access and exchange based on a "need-to-know basis" less of a privilege. Greater opportunities for personal expression and broader comprehension by all workers will continue to increase. Consider, prior to the advent of television, most Americans had to travel to get a good appreciation of different lifestyles. Informational relatedness is an individual's consciousness, including facts, feelings, perceptions, beliefs, values, personality, and expectations. Unfairness, greed, immorality, laziness, arrogance, envy, deceit, stupidity, and the other soiled baggage persons carry about will not remain outside the organization. Therefore, arriving at business clarity is much easier when framed from a business standpoint than a personal one.

Today, popular opinion tells us that youngsters and adult workers as a whole seem less disciplined and more stressed than those of previous generations. No longer does "prescribed leadership" impart confidence on the basis of its title, because individuals are using more informational-relatedness in discerning a broader array of choices. The worker is thinking more about their own perceptions and situation while living an ever-increasing life experience. This does not mean persons today are necessarily better thinkers than those of former generations, only that they have more to clarify in their thinking. On the wall of a chief executive's office a plaque hung:

> We May Play Golf and
> We May Dine and
> I Am Happy to Call
> You My Friend
> But When It Comes
> Down to Business
> It Stands Alone

When asked what it meant, she replied, "Years ago, when I was a regional VP, a new marketing manager brought me a proposal. After much discussion and deliberation, the company invested in his 'Secret Shopper Drawing' campaign, where persons who bought the company's product would have a chance to win some prizes. My region was the test pilot, and if the campaign were successful in getting new customers, it would be rolled out nationally. We heavily advertised and promoted a short marketing campaign. The customer simply filled out a form and mailed it back to the marketing department to be entered for a future drawing. Marketing had announced that customers' entries numbered in the thousands. A huge, decorated box filled with replies was ceremoniously presented, with top national executives and the winners in attendance for the grand drawing. Everyone was pleased with the announced outcome. As it turned out, the big success was a bust. I received an anonymous tip after the drawing. The note said that the big box had an elevated hidden bottom. The number of customer entries was small, the majority being repeat-entries from a couple hundred customers. Obviously, the marketing manager wanted desperately to be recognized for some achievement. His proposal's success would have probably earned him more responsibility, recognition, and reward. However, what is desirable for my business must stem from an unbiased perspective. How are things to be accomplished in the best possible way? Self-aggrandizement follows sound business, and not vice versa. That's what that message on the wall means." Conducting business internally or externally requires the primary execution of those actions that protect, maintain, and/or improve business in the best way.

On a bright, sun shiny weekend morning, the boys ask, "Can we go out to play?" Mom and Dad reply, "Not until your room is clean." Less than an hour later, it is time for inspection. Dad goes to the bedroom door and takes a peek. "Straighten out your beds a little better and dust the furniture," he commands. A few minutes later, Mom arrives. She drops to one knee and looks under the beds, opens the closet door, and opens the clothes drawers. "You guys aren't going anywhere until you clean out from under your beds, separate your clean clothes from the dirty ones, straighten out your closet, get your drawers in order, and vacuum." Mom leaves, and one brother says to the other, "See, I told you it wouldn't work." The children had one thing on their minds, and that was to go outside and play sooner rather than later. The parents each had a different perspective on what should have been accomplished as well. The reactive natures of human interaction and a lack of clarity can be evident at the most intimate and elementary levels of social interaction.

This concept of clarifying what is intended from a business perspective has little to do with assessing what value means from the standpoint of the employee, as the aim desired from the employee's behavior. Whether considering the tire company, the prize drawing, or the children example, outcomes were evaluated from a personal frame of reference.

Mind reading is not an option. Is the intent of the job interview to employ someone to do a job or hire someone that the interviewer 'feels' comfortable with? It is suggested that feelings lurking in darkness pose too difficult a reach for either interviewer or applicant to grasp, and that hiring decisions must attend to what's mutually apparent.

Incorrect information has as much merit as accurate information when communicating. A lie or incorrect assumption accepted as truth *is* truth. Moving like grains of sand passing through a sieve, some information falls freely, while other bits cling to the sieve's interior, all seemingly undistinguishable from one another. Upon closer examination, all the granules display an array of size, texture, composition, and shape. Job interviews should be designed to sift through applicant information to find and examine distinguishing features beyond feelings of affability, affinity, or concurrence. Understandably, that which sticks or doesn't stick can have more to do with the sieve than the content passing through it. **Traditional job interviewing does not clarify applicant selection because it is conducted on the basis of subjective ambiguities.**

Business Expectations

Management's philosophy, decision-making, policies, and conduct outside of protected civil rights are an organization's prerogative. The employee who becomes overly frustrated and resentful because of status quo imperfections should recall, consider, and affirm their motivations for accepting employment in the first place and then decide to stay or move on. The organization factors compensation in relation to labor time, activities, and/or results, but not employee satisfaction. In contrast, promoting employee job satisfaction is important to organizations as a means of reducing voluntary labor turnover cost. Thus, whether the applicant can do the job and desires the job are based upon defining job content first, or what the job requires in terms of the employer's desired KSA's. An employee's job success, however, is therefore a function of organizational management and employee performance.

> The behavior of any organizational performer is the product of motivational forces that derive in large part from the behavior of members of his role set.... Each position in an organization is directly related to certain others, less directly to still others and perhaps remotely connected to fewer others. These pressures induce in an employee an experience which has both opinionated and factual properties, and which leads in turn to certain adaptive (or maladaptive) responses. Those exerting the pressures observe responses in the employee. In turn, the observers' expectations are correspondingly adjusted. Thus a work episode involves experience and response by both an employee and others. Successful organizational change poses difficulties.

We purpose that these difficulties are due in part to the persistent utilization of the wrong unit for achieving change; the concentration has been on the individual when it should be on the role set.... To remove a person from his role set, tell him in a training program or executive interview that he should change his behavior, and then return him to the unchanged set burdens him with a double responsibility. He must not only change his own behavior; he must effect complementary changes in the expectations and behavior of his role set senders. This is the characteristic and crucial weakness shared by conventional programs of training, communications, and executive exhortation. (Kahn et.al., 1964, 35, 396)

As the role set increases in member size, expectations, or managerial dominance, the potential for "organizational or comfortable fit" becomes a more ambiguous concept. Psychological stresses among employees, such as frustration and anxiety, can occur. Organizations don't behave; only individuals within them do. Bennis wrote, "...an organization can be a judgmental place in which those who do not share the common set, the common view, are by definition deviant, marginal outsiders... The fact that the organizational deviant... may be the institution's vital and only link with some new, more apt paradigm does not make the organization value that person any more. Most organizations would rather risk obsolescence than make room for the nonconformist in their midst" (1989, 124). Nothing in business is more uncomfortable for most individuals than not knowing how they should fit in during the traditional interviewing session. Their expectation is to meet the interviewer's expectation, thereby getting a job offer. But what does the interviewer expect, not in terms of an employee, but an applicant? Just as employee behavior can be affected by role set and expectations, no applicant wants to be at odds with the interviewer's expectations. **Traditional job interviewing is obsolete because what's expected from applicants is hidden from them, and it does not automatically adjust to different applicants seeking the same job.**

Considering the sensibility of business concerns can be complex due to the diverse natures of people. Fortunately, the business organization was never intended to be all things to all persons it may employ. Knowing where you are going is more important than knowing where you came from. If standing blindfolded at the edge of a cliff, wouldn't you want your next step not to be your last one? Although stepping into a job interview is never lethal, the outcome is important and typically urgent. Applicants are not blind to job interviewing risks, but they should be able to see clearly the interview's landscape before proceeding. Employers should make clear what they are looking for from a prospective employee. Every job interview carries uncertain outcomes for both.

The interviewer is the applicant's guide. A good guide understands what's needed, plans, and maps the route to arrive at a destination on time. A poor guide does the opposite of those things, while failing to lead with the correct purpose of mind. This purpose is to arrive at a reasoned determination on which applicant shows the best capability to fulfill the employer's expectations while allowing every applicant to take part in the trip. Since those they are leading don't know exactly where they are headed or what they may need, it is up to the interviewer to be clear on this matter. Applicants can only rely on the interviewer's lead. As will be shown, the necessary tasks and behaviors to conduct a successful interview session can be easily learned and developed by interviewers. Short of a frontal lobotomy, overcoming those subjective impulses that make all of us who we are as individuals would be impossible. It is not a question of good or bad intentions, but of how such impulses can influence decision-making in the wrong direction. Rather than overcoming subjectivity or bias completely, diminishing their influence during the job interview can be a significant improvement and painless.

3
Interviewer Concerns

Mature job applicants are not seeking adoption or foster care from another adult. Metaphorically, it is easy to speak of business in socially-recognizable or appealing expressions, but one is also not volunteering to embrace some selfless cause when seeking paid employment. They know that they are willing, ready, and able to provide a business service at some level. However, their work capabilities often remain hidden within their individual packaging because the interviewer fails to pull away the wrapping to see a prospective employee. Figure 3-1 shows that the typical job interview can only be realized from independent viewpoints. No matter how badly the employer wants a good employee or an individual wants employment, this awkward activity is based on interviewer and applicant subjectivity, but not an interactive business process evaluating job performance needs, leaving both the interviewer and interviewee with the misguided intent of trying to establish personal familiarity. What does a good interview mean? From the applicant's perspective, it would mean getting an offer for employment, and from the employer's viewpoint, this would mean getting an employee that will provide the best work.

Unfortunately, with the typical job interview as depicted in Figure 3-1, business perspectives are a lesser priority and less developed concern for both interviewer and job-seeker. Silent protocols and communicative exchange are the first consideration and are of higher importance for both on a social level. This emphasis will hold whether the interviewer is the ultimate decision-maker in hiring or not, because anticipation of and adherence to customarily understood social protocols shape each participant's expectations and behaviors towards one another in traditional interviews. Mutually serious considerations about relevant business matters are largely ignored due to an urgent emptiness between interviewer and applicant. Social possibilities, those ending in subjective clarity and certitude about longer-term relationships yet begun, fill the void—"Can we get along?", "Are they sincere?", "How are they interpreting me?"—leaving the essential purpose of the interview to a vacillating and awkward activity, but not a process for assessing degrees of future employee capability.

Figure 3-1
TRADITIONAL INTERVIEW PERCEPTIONS

HIGHER IMPORTANCE

Employer's Focus	**Interviewer's Focus**	**Applicant's Focus**
High Subjectivity On the Job	High Subjectivity On the Applicant	High Subjectivity On the Interviewer
▲	▲	▲
Primary Interest	Primary Interest	Primary Interest
▲	▼	▼
Future Business Benefits	Future Business Work	Future Business Work

LOWER IMPORTANCE

An informal phone survey of twenty-seven interviewers and recruiters posed the following question: "Based on your experience, what are the most frequent challenges you face when preparing or conducting job interviews with applicants?" Five answers by them, beginning with the most frequent given, are as follows:

- Getting an applicant to open up.
- Getting applicants to "be themselves." (What does this mean?)
- Providing "good" questions for applicants to answer.
- Finding distinguishing characteristics that separate applicants from one another.
- Remembering reasons for comparisons between applicants.

Does the applicant care whether the interviewer likes him or her? You bet they do. But the problem is that the applicant wants to be liked for the wrong reason—the interview. This emphatic, unknown reliance by applicants on an interviewer's challenges and what's important to the interviewer encourages conflicted reasoning and actions, leading to the preposterous proposition for applicants of explaining one's literal self. Ninety percent of books on job interviewing are written to help job-seekers. Note, they are not written to help them perform as employees or do work for hire. They have been written to help them land employment or pass the selection process. "Well, there's a highly competitive labor market out there, and applicants have to make the best impression" is the typical justification raised in defense of one's ability to present well. If that's the case, employers must be more interested in interview presentation performances because it is a good indicator of what an applicant's future job performance will be. However, this would only be true for positions like sales or counseling, where the abilities of being persuasive (winning) and empathizing are primary. Do employers want all applicants to be salespersons first and foremost? Great salespeople can sell a bad thing as effectively as they can a good thing. Poor ones go hungry. Those who come to the interview prepared in other ways, perhaps as cooks, would find it very difficult to serve up an organization's essential diet. In light of this, it seems more likely that an employer could be subjected to a real hunger. The other ten percent of books on job interviewing are written for employers and interviewers on how to find and better select employees. One hundred percent of interviewing books are about finding a mutually beneficial business arrangement! Why should the applicant and interviewer consider anything but real aspects of the future business opportunity, since that is the real hunger for both? A manager once remarked that a particular job candidate's credentials and tests of ability were very outstanding, but he decided not hire him. His reason was simpleminded: the candidate stuttered. If the applicant had been hired, he was destined to work in the accounting department, crunching numbers all day with little opportunity for extensive discourse.

An interview session can be similar to the scene depicted in "Goldilocks and the Three Bears" with the bowls of porridge, in that what's "just right" is a matter of taste and not substance. Yet the applicant does not sit for an interview uninvited, and it is unlikely that they will be given a second and third opportunity to get it right. Why is he or she there: to present correctly or show a willingness and readiness to perform a job? As argued, their true intent is not to form a personal bond with the organization or interviewer. In the absence of substantive and factual subject matter, what other course is left to the interviewer and applicant but to forage aimlessly for some social appeal? In this instance, interview presentation is like being served dessert instead of a meal. Though hastily consumed and maybe tasty, it is certainly not the proper sustenance for one's workdays. Since making an employment determination is the intent of this business encounter, those who host such events for a living may find the following interviewer etiquette helpful in maintaining the correct focus.

- Assume your guest was not born yesterday.
- Assume your guest only enjoys talking about things you hate.
- Assume your guest would prefer to be somewhere else or with someone else.
- Assume the two of you will never share personal time together.

Later it will be shown that these assumptions, coupled with other proper procedures, will provide a highly professional business encounter. It is a business process for accomplishing the employer's interview objective that has three aspects—adaptability, efficiency, and quality—while also forcing the applicant to make an effort that is demonstrative of a sincere interest in accomplishing business beforehand, rather than "giving the business" after being hired. After all, they will be paid to accomplish things on the employer's behalf and not their own.

Interviewer's Abilities

The most competent job interviewers have the following abilities:

- Can define essential work behaviors needed for a position.
- Can create and manipulate "free space" to gauge mental work behaviors.
- Can structure questions in proper context.
- Can distinguish between workplace conduct and work performance issues.

- Can recognize that testing applicants for specific abilities may be appropriate.

- Can evaluate and distinguish applicants and not individuals, using a high degree of objective information.

- Can host a stranger with tact and diplomacy to lessen applicant posturing and anxiety.

Unlike most organizational activities, the selection of new employees occurs sporadically and is commonly conducted as a single businessperson's closed and solitary affair. Other business activities, such as accounting and customer service, run more openly and routinely. Thereby, receiving consistent organizational oversight and objective feedback either directly or coincidentally. Loafing, shoddiness, inaccuracies, complaints, and so forth can be quite apparent, acting as warning signs to management that something is amiss. Although written aptitude and ability test scores, or interviewing by committee, may be used to gain a more objective appraisal of individual applicants, typical interview practices are not subject to uniform standards of conduct, observation, or even random review to better clarify why one applicant was chosen over another, leaving interviews and subsequent assessments of prospective employees particularly prone to carelessness and error.

Those left only to self-counsel may be ill-advised, but are never wrong. Personal or organizational sizing of individuals as persons, as opposed to applicants, is an impractical interviewing measure. Attempting assessments based on hope represents not only a waste of time to all parties, but also a disservice to the unsuccessful applicant, the interviewer, and the employer. Employers hire for work support, individuals work for living support, and interviewers support joint work opportunities between the two. This means that the most required for any job is the least needed to accomplish a job. The best of that depends on recognizing and evaluating that which is required, and then selecting individuals that can specifically meet those requirements overall. How can interviewers improve upon their technique without knowing how to proceed and without analyzing pertinent evidence? How do organizations know that interviewers are conducting interviews properly and choosing the best future worker? Contrary to the VP of Human Resources mentioned earlier, interviewers do produce results (choices), and it would be wise to manage as effectively as possible the selection of new employees.

Interpersonal Communications

Verbal communication skills are not less or more significant than other job skills, but they can easily mask those other skills or the fact that other needed skills are not present in the applicant. Kinesics is the study of body movements, facial expressions, gaze, and gestures as nonverbal signals used as means of communication. Interestingly, Birdwhistell (1970) has offered the following regarding the smile and communication. The smile as a facial gesture is not necessarily an expression of pleasure or pleasantness. It is both culturally defined and variable in meaning depending on hidden motives and circumstances. A smile may be displayed to indicate an involuntary reflex, humor, ridicule, doubt, good manners, superiority, acceptance, subordination, friendliness, deception, insult, and/or a denial of insult. So, a smile's signal value is debatable, thus interpretive. Communication is not to be found only in gesture or the smaller set of vocal features such as voice quality, loudness, and tempo, any more than it can be discovered in words alone.

Mimicry and synchrony, not to be confused with manners, are very common nonverbal language responses which people consciously or unconsciously display, especially when faced with unusual or uncertain interpersonal occasions (Hatfield et al., 1994). Funerals, interviews, and parties are some typical events where such body language serves to maintain social balance, given the dominant situational theme. Successful salespeople and other emotional workers learn to control their own nonverbal signals and read those sent by others, in a conscious effort to control the social balance between themselves and their customers or clients in order to accomplish their own work agendas. The emotional vibes that an interviewer projects may be conducive to an emotional climate that is contrary to an applicant's intentions or, more importantly, counterproductive to the business at hand (Baron 1993). An applicant's attempt to be in synchrony or connected with an interviewer's projected but inappropriately-expressed mood may result in confusion and emotional discomfort for both (Siegman and Reynolds 1982; Cappella and Palmer 1990).

Bosses who habitually display emotional outbursts by demeaning their subordinates do so because to make a rational appeal about the matter at hand is extremely difficult, leaving such misbehavior a handy crutch for them within the organization. Unlike rational finesse, which a competent emotional worker may use to get results, intimidation does not demonstrate an ability to persuade, but is simply dominance. Lessons learned from this naked drama, which any small child might explain, "Be careful what you say," "Don't make mistakes," "Don't get caught," and "All I need is power to be right." The irony in this is that many mature adults at work will swallow the latter lesson to be "in sync," but in doing so, serious thinking and discovery is left unattended. In one respect, though, it is fortunate for the organization that most mature adults typically will avoid expressions of rational criticism and confrontation towards superiors. Such controlled reactions assist in minimizing the eruption of chaos in the workplace.

Kloman (1967) gave evidence that black and white job applicants behaved quite differently non-verbally, although their intent was the same. White job candidates tended to frequently nod or say "Uh-huh" to acknowledge interviewer's remarks, whereas black applicants gave no visible gestures, which led the interviewers to believe they were not paying close attention. A study by Rosenthal (1974) found that older people are more sensitive to nonverbal signals than younger people. If Harrison's (1965) analysis is correct, a person receives 65% of messages sent through means other than words. On what basis are most job interviews judged? "Our non-verbals of whatever kind, conscious or unconscious, may be characterized as follows: they communicate something, they are believed, they are situation-bound, they are seldom isolated, and they affect our relationships" (Ross, R. and Ross, M., 1982, 200).

Subjective probing for irrelevancies or "hidden factors" by an interviewer will skew the selection process in favor of more gregarious candidates. Those who are more persuasive as campaigners, talkers, and presenters are better equipped to establish rapport. Rapport means to be in harmony with another and, as will hopefully be made clear, communicating effectively around a business theme requires more than harmony.

Irrelevancies

A speaker once remarked, "One of the most important aspects in the interview process is gauging the applicant's desire for longevity with the firm. Therefore, I always ask applicants how they view their future through a series of open-ended questions. After all, when we hire someone, it is an investment in their future and ours through training and the like. It only makes sense to achieve a higher return on investment through an extended employee service period." The audience had paid over three hundred and fifty dollars a head to hear such presumptive reasoning, and a fortuneteller could have provided as much insight for twenty bucks.

It is neither appropriate nor necessary for job applicants to be subjected to irrelevant and unwarranted questions, which lead to assumptions about the person, rather than attempting to predict future worker capability. Whether an interviewer is being nosy, needs to fill time, or really thinks that such information is pertinent to their hiring assessment, the applicant's salary history, ambitions, hobbies, dreams, values, future, and the like are not the interviewer's or the company's business. Suppose they want the interviewer's or future boss's job? Is such an ambition bad or in poor taste? Isn't such a desire really a form of flattery? Since the interviewee is promoting himself or herself, it is ludicrous to ask them to imitate that which could be easily misconstrued. After his son won a Cub Scout model car derby competition, a father humorously commented, "When I was boy, my father and I competed in this event, and we never got close to a win. I didn't think I had what it takes to build a simple box. Wow, the top winner! I'm glad my son was born; he's done wonders for my self-esteem." Because someone hasn't, does not mean they can't.

> Discrepancy between expression (of the speaker) and impression (of the listener) is the normal state of affairs and that we are bound to misunderstand

extremely important aspects of human relations if we fail to take these ever present, basic discrepancies fully into account.... The expectation that there is some kind of "natural harmony," or even complete identity, between expression and impression is based on the silent assumption that the mechanisms of expression and those of impression are somehow, in a predetermined way, attuned to each other.... *Between the inner personality, its attitudes, sentiments, and tendencies, and the external personality there is always a certain degree of incongruity. In human relations we have always to suppress, or at least modify, the frank expression of some factors.* (Ichheiser, G., 1970, 18-19, italics added)

Biases

Many interviewers are inclined to go about their job as anyone who makes casual inquiries to someone would. Such inquiry can be compared to that of strangers meeting for the first time. They may or may not develop "chemistry." The irony is that the job interview is not a coincidental or casual occurrence. On both sides of the table are strangers whose only purpose for meeting is to conduct serious business. It has been demonstrated that people reveal a common bias when trying to judge someone else's behavior. They tend to overestimate personality traits and underestimate the influence of the situation (Forgas 1998). Psychological studies have also concluded the following:

People within a single culture tend to label persons by particular behaviors and attributes (Manz and Lueck 1968). For example, people who wear glasses or possess credentials may to be judged as more intelligent than those without.

People tend to have ideas about what traits are related to or go with other traits to form larger networks of relationships (Schneider 1973; Berman and Kenny 1976). For example, a man might presume that a woman wearing scantily provocative attire is also promiscuous. Young Einstein was considered ignorant of a perceived social etiquette—deference to authority. These extensions of thought go way beyond the actual information at hand and constitute prejudice.

A person's first impressions are the strongest and lead to categorization. Having formed a category, contradictory new information is given less attention (Luchins 1957; Nisbett and Ross 1980). Young Einstein spoke of relativity, not relatives: "So-and-so likes to gossip' therefore, she undermines morale." Thus, small samples of observations are given high representative weight (Kahneman and Tversky 1973).

What a person believes and expects about another person may affect how that other person begins to act in turn (Snyder 1979; Snyder and Swann 1978). A new department manager was curious why one worker among thirteen subordinates always provided hard-copy drafts of special assignments rather than emailing them. He would write comments and questions on the submittals and then return them to the workers for further revisions. For convenience, the manager preferred an electronic draft, as done by the other subordinates. When the manager asked the employee why he handled assignments in that way, the following response was given: "Well, sir, I realize that all of us are getting paid to work, but I feel my ideas and imagination are premiums. I may be wrong, but handing them to you in hard copy allows me to feel a sense of continual ownership and a certain degree of control. Hopefully, I will receive some credit if my work has merit while moving up the chain." This employee's work behavior was a result of a negative bias (he didn't trust the manager or office politics) in view of a perceived positive expectation (recognition/rewards). The manager did not request a change in this employee's particular work behavior. He remained receptive because creative outcomes were more important to him than convenience. But the thought of how much creativity or innovation from other subordinates could be lost because of similar thinking now gave the manager a new concern.

Comprehension

Interviewers must be mindful of their limitations as "subject matter experts" also. A firm is seeking to fill the following vacancies: software engineer, supervisor, secretary, janitor, and salesperson. What is the interviewer's background or familiarity with these positions? Assume the interviewer has no experience in any of these roles. If the interviewer were to interview qualified applicants for these positions, the applicant that would probably impress them the most would be the salesperson. This is because the qualified salesperson is prepared to persuade and convince—that's their realm. Other candidates may find it more difficult to impress because personal communication technique may be less developed. Moreover, mutual experiences and expectations between a less-informed interviewer and a qualified applicant are more distant, causing a kind of perceptual distortion that may occur in any interpersonal situation and thus minimize rapport. Naturally, this is a more frequent occurrence when the interview sessions are staggered and a first interview is used to screen applicants before allowing them access to a more seasoned subject matter expert.

An applicant saw a recruitment ad for a high-tech firm and sent a cover letter and resume requesting an interview. The senior human resource manager had been directed by the CEO to take an active lead in searching for and screening highly-qualified candidates for a specific position opening. This applicant's credentials were of particular interest to the company. The resume indicated the applicant was a Ph.D. candidate who had published several academic papers about computer software. When the candidate arrived for his interview, he was dressed oddly with a small head covering and had a long beard.

He appeared to have stepped off a plane that had flown non-stop from the Middle East. During the brief interview, the applicant asked where he could perform prayers and inquired about company accommodations that would allow him to participate in other religious observations. Subsequently, this American applicant did not receive a job offer. Several months later, the same applicant met one of his former professors at a computer science convention. That professor suggested the student apply for a job at the same company that had previously rejected him. Some time after the convention, the professor, who was a private consultant for the same firm, contacted the CEO to determine how the company had lost an opportunity to hire this person, who subsequently gained employment elsewhere. The CEO, based on the professor's concerns and information, called the human resource manager to discuss why the applicant was not offered the position. The manager informed the CEO that this candidate would be a distraction to other employees, would require higher maintenance, and would not fit into the company's culture. The CEO replied that oddity diminishes with familiarity, that by decency and law we accommodate special needs, and that this was not a commune but "my business." Subsequently, the CEO requested the manager's resignation.

Failures in the understanding of what's important are not due just to faulty judgment, but may also result from plain ignorance. It is well documented that "noise," which is here defined as meaning unwanted or undesirable (unpleasant or bothersome) sound, can impair task performance. Some people can concentrate with the radio on, while others find it distracting. Librarians prohibit talking above certain levels. According to Broadbent (1979), tasks that require a person to keep track of two processes at the same time are made more difficult by noise. He further explains how the arousal concept regarding noise can interfere with work. Work in itself increases a person's arousal level. Noise at certain levels further increases an individual's arousal level beyond an optimum or normal level. To compensate, the person narrows their attention and focus, thus ignoring irrelevant stimuli. As arousal level increases even more, the person's attention becomes narrower, and other essential work considerations and/or actions are ignored. In complex tasks, noise creates a work overload (Broadbent 1971).

Broadbent's work has implications for applicants and employees. If the task or work is complex or highly focused, do the working conditions support the outcomes expected? For example, one cannot wear earplugs during a meeting. It is an acknowledged fact that outside of a group meeting, certain workers seem to express themselves better. Perhaps the noise of others talking during their thinking is bothersome or distracting and causes a mental overload? Given the job, are special worker characteristics or work considerations needed? Meetings with an informative purpose can be easily attended and appreciated by most. Interactive work meetings requiring attention and concentration to derive decisions and outcomes can make certain employees appear as loafers when in fact they are not.

To hear (sensory), to think (interpret and evaluate), and to verbally respond (send what message) are three complex and independent processes which are self-regulated.

Broadbent's research and the commonly observed "cocktail party phenomenon," where an individual normally focuses on just one conversation, ignoring other distractions in a room, indicate that one's perception can be selective, yet responsiveness can be slow. The quality or type of an individual's responses to an interviewer may have more to do with individual arousals and selective perceptions in the judgements of both as well as time constraints rather than an inability to grasp the importance or particular significance of an expressed interview topic.

Structured Interview Types

Structured job interviews are the standard and accepted method upon which interviewing is currently based. It is a planned approach where prewritten interviewer's questions are used for collecting information from applicants and that information is then used in selecting future employees. Findings have shown that a structured job interview, due to its standardization of questions, can provide higher reliability and potential validity than an unstructured interview or those where the interviewer makes up questions at will (Huffcutt and Arthur 1994; McDaniel et al. 1994). Furthermore, better predictability of future job performance through measures of job knowledge or general cognitive ability has also been documented from traditional structured formats (Gottfredson 1986; Hunter 1986). As a tool for selecting new employees and predicting their future work success, this format could be improved dramatically. Three versions described below are based on the structured interview, but each has inherent weaknesses in reasonableness, efficiency, and value.

Biographical/Behavioral (BB) profiling and typing is the oldest and most commonly used job interview technique. It is based on the belief that an applicant's past experiences and interpersonal attractiveness are an adequate indicator for picking a good employee. It is highly interviewer-centered and places undue emphasis on the perception of an applicant's immutable disposition, while minimizing capability assessments and ignoring factors inherent in the interview session itself. In addition, it assumes an applicant's past work performance, whether outstanding or mediocre, happened in a vacuum, meaning that previous opportunity and circumstance played little or no part in the applicant's past performance.

The situational and critical incident interviews are the most recent versions of the structured interview and are "somewhat" more applicant-centered. Initially introduced by academics and psychologists to provide a better alternative to the BB, they are complicated to construct, conduct, and evaluate, which makes their interpretation and utility by laypersons suspect. The situational interview is conducted by using prepared situational statements. The interviewer asks the applicant to respond to a series of short statements by describing how they have or would act given the situation presented. A series of these statements is orally presented to the applicant individually, and responses are noted. An applicant's reply may or may not be rated against predetermined answers. A major flaw in this method is that in the interest of fairness, the interviewer must take the position that all applicants have the same presence of mind (selective attention/personal interest) for the situations posed as they would for the overall job. A simple analogy illustrates the fallacy of that assumption. When shopping for a car, a buyer may not have a particular interest in some features, but the car is still purchased. From the interviewer's standpoint, the expressed situation given is most important; but to the applicant's mind, it may be of minimal concern and given scant consideration. The interviewer and applicant may be judging and responding to limited bits of information outside of a mutual frame of reference. Clearly, a factual work situation is not present.

In the critical incident interviewing technique, the applicant is given a situation or topic, e.g. "You have been given a deadline to complete an important assignment. You have repeatedly asked for vital information from a coworker in a different department, and you have no authority over her. She keeps putting you off and your deadline is approaching (the critical incident). What will you do?" Or the applicant is asked to describe a past work episode in detail related to that topic and explain how they handled it. Here again, such an approach has dubious value in predicting future applicant performance, because the job-seeker has no notion of an actual context. A lack of cooperation and a looming deadline would seem to indicate that some trial and error actions (work) would be prudent as opposed to an instant plan for action. The applicant's response is constrained by aspects of comprehending the question in narrow or broad terms, remembering, and the lack of props that may be able to help support effective decisions and actions in real life. Moreover, the available time that is thought to remain for responding is more significant to the applicant than the situation posed. Yet, most importantly, in spite of these factors, the applicant is expected to provide an acceptable answer, and not a reasoned response.

In each of the more recent interviewing techniques, attempts are being made to better judge critical thinking in an applicant. Realistically, only quick, non-reflective thought can be realized from such approaches. Even more deficiencies are present in these typical interview practices, which diminish opportunities for properly evaluating and selecting new employees.

Mischaracterizations are not what interviewers intend as they attempt to select individuals to become employees. Psychologists can readily become interviewers, and it has been demonstrated that they are able to perform better assessments of applicants (Gaugler et al. 1987). This advantage probably has more to do with their practiced approach of emotional detachment and assessing bits of information more critically than a layperson normally would. Requiring those who conduct job interviews to be psychologists is neither practical nor necessary. Hidden meanings, personality typing, non-work behaviors, communicative patterns, and so forth cannot be easily comprehended or evaluated by the untrained. The solution is simple. Interviewers should not bother trying to assess such factors in the first place.

4
Preparing Interview Content

Creating a climate that contributes to job-relevant information sharing serves the applicant, employee, and employer by identifying work-related judgments and actions that are germane to the business environment. Some employers lament lackluster profits, productivity, quality, and customer service, while their employees wonder aloud, "What should we be doing that we're not doing?" As a lyric in a popular Bob Dylan song goes, "The answer, my friend, is blowing in the wind…." Smoke is difficult to capture, let alone make sense of. The smoke and mirrors of the well-known job interview must now be discarded. It is essential that a new interview process must support business transactions while minimizing the entry of non-business subjectivities.

Job Interviewing as Business Process

Must clarify and integrate all functional roles and components for the following in seamless fashion:
- Any Employer
- Any Applicant
- Any Interviewer
- Any Job
- Collecting Information
- Assessing
- Standards
- Practicality

While minimizing the entry of:
- Biases
- Speculations
- Irrelevancies
- Ambiguities
- Dominance
- Misunderstandings

Process Elements

Any business process contains elements on a controlled pathway towards a specified outcome. All business processes are deemed successful based on three conditions: adaptability, efficiency, and quality. Depending on the degree of adaptability, business processes can perform broader functions and adjust to fit different demands. Efficiency is a measure of cost per time to arrive at a particular quality standard. The three distinct elements of the interview process are interviewer(s), applicant information, and the job being considered. Once this interviewing process is fulfilled and a new employee is hired, a new process is created with the following elements: management, employee (former applicant), and job outcomes. Future work performances can be most significantly impacted by two singular dependent variables: interviewers and management. Dependent variables to a process are factors that can be controlled. The information sought and what is desired in terms of work are within the power of the interviewer and management to obtain and express. Applicant information is an independent variable in the process because as a factor, it may differ among applicants. Employee work performance is also an independent variable due to an employee's independent work behaviors. If at the onset, interviewers falter due to their performance or an inadequate process, then management could pay a higher-than-necessary cost to arrive at quality work outcomes. The interview process may only serve the following organizational needs:

- To validate a candidate's qualifications.
- To sort perspective candidates into specific categories for promoting organizational diversity.
- To determine if the candidate has the necessary prerequisite skills and capability to perform as needed.
- To determine which candidate will be offered the job.

Role Play

Many organizations approach job placement or employee selection from the standpoint of a general appraisal based on a job title. This fosters a vague position description whereby the interviewer presumes undefined skills are present or absent in the applicant, which more often than not results in a superficial impression of the job and candidate. "We need a manager, and this is what a manager should be." "We need a laborer, and this is what a laborer should be." Would the role of a telemarketing manager be different than the role of a shipyard worker? Would the role of a manufacturing assembly line worker be different than a customer service phone manager? Could any one of these persons successfully perform any of the others' jobs? The question is not what one should be, but what one can do. Any of those workers could be successful at the other's job, as could any person perform any occupation provided they possess the needed enabling abilities and desire. Actors and actresses masquerade purposely as characters, while other workers perform activities as themselves. Saying, "I am a doctor, lawyer, plumber, manager, et cetera" is an abbreviation for what persons do for a livelihood and not who they are.

Interviews provide opportunities for diversity to be planted within an organization. Gender and race are visible characteristics, yet diversity itself is an organizational hybrid blended of many unique individual attributes. As applicants try to play the role of best interviewee, they unwittingly undermine an organization's desire to achieve viable diversity. Knowledge, experiences, philosophies, passions, and other aspects of individualism serve to enrich the business landscape. Organizations, therefore, should protect against erosion to their soil by cultivating applicant thinking during the interview session. Burying interviewees beneath arrogant and self-righteous matter that is foreign and nonessential to an organization's productive harvest can smother fertile growth.

Defining Expectations

Conducting a proper job interview requires proper preparation. The preparation prior to the actual face-to-face is the most labor-intensive aspect of the interviewing process. Businesses large and small typically shortcut this critical area because it requires discernment, application, and review—it is laborious work. Regardless of whether the position to be filled requires soft skills (general) or hard skills (specific), what will be termed the "position profile" determines the organization's interest and is the foundation of a new interview process.

What does an organization want an applicant to do after being hired? Do a little or a lot? Be prepared to handle crisis? Execute even workloads or stand-alone assignments? Meet variable deadlines, or maintain consistent workflow? Use a great deal of personal initiative and autonomy, or follow prescribed procedures? Give written reports or verbal? Do emotional work? To what degree? Demonstrate creativity, or work in a box? Be politically constrained, or manage objectively? Type twenty words a minute or eighty? Use certain types of computer software or paper and pencil? Is overtime customary? Get results? If so, what criteria is used to measure them? If an organization cannot produce a written "position profile" for every unique position within the organization, there exists no proof for the position. Before the reader dismisses such an assertion as nonsense, consider the following.

Jane Doe works tireless hours for her employer, and although there is no profile for her position, she can show the fruits of her labor to anyone who's interested. Ms. Doe leaves her employer. Does the employer then run an ad that says, "Now Hiring for J. Doe's Work"? Organizations must get beyond the personal (someone's mind) by doing a better job of clarifying their needs and expectations.

For instance, the difference between being politically constrained (quasi or true emotional work) and managing objectively can spark confusion as well as conflict within and around personnel. If a job position requires the taking and supporting of sides on an issue(s), then conformity to what may be a personally objectionable viewpoint is a vital prerequisite for the job from the employer's perspective. Having a mouthpiece is more important than objective thinking, and that message must come across loud and clear in the interview. Appointees of elected officials are prime examples of such prescribed expectations. Using a properly prepared position profile elevates critical and essential expectations for the employer and applicant. Osburn, Timmreck, and Bigby (1981) found job-relevant information of a specific, rather than general, description allows interviewers to differentiate between applicants more effectively.

Clarifying Objectives

Instructional technologists and designers employ, among other things, a highly-structured technique known as job analysis to develop instructional packages, curricula, and courses. This methodology can be applied to any job activity imaginable where behavioral aspects of an activity can be described and sequenced. The specificity of using this type of analysis can reduce the behavioral components, or how one does something, into very small elements. For example, the job of preparing a can of hot soup can require over twenty-five distinct behavioral elements, depending on whether a particular can must be found and identified, what type of can opener will be used, whether a microwave or conventional stove is to be used, etc. The reader may have a better appreciation of developing this analysis by imagining that it is being made for a person who doesn't speak or read English and has lived off the land their entire life. Applying such rigor in the design and development of instructional content is a necessary exercise in evaluating and determining the best instructional design strategy based on a learner's characteristics. In developing a position profile, such precision would prove cumbersome and add little to the profile's overall effectiveness as an interviewer and applicant assessment tool. Although the following is based on job analysis technique, it is not identical in definition or application. The position profile states the desired work expectations and provides a means of inferring those work behaviors needed in accomplishing them.

In creating and developing a position profile, begin with the actual objectives, outcomes, goals and/or intents that are to be accomplished by one employee. If a position's incumbent is already achieving the open position's aims, record those through observation and discussion. Specificity of distinct job objectives is critical. If the position is newly created, the first question to be answered should be what is expected from the position in broad terms—the vision. The vision is then analyzed and broken down into narrower statements called job objectives. What should someone in the position be able to accomplish? The importance in distinction between vision and accomplishment is illustrated in the following motivational parable.

Three brick-masons were plying their trade. Each was asked what they were doing. One mason responded, "I am laying brick." Another responded, "I am building a wall." The third responded, "I am building a cathedral." The intended conclusion to be drawn from this parable is that the third mason expressed a greater vision for his task and thus should be motivated to perform better. Now, if the third mason was an atheist, should the same intent be drawn? Vision is not a substitute for performance. Robert Mager's outstanding book *Goal Analysis* is an invaluable reference tool for writing clear goals and mentions, "…the object of analysis is to figure out how to know an outcome when you see one, not to make one happen."

"The position will increase sales" is not a statement of a work objective, but a statement of work vision. "The position will increase sales (what's to be done) by 5% within six months (when it's to be done)" is a proper statement of a work outcome. Any statement of outcome will by definition have two parts: the descriptive phrase and a conditional clause. "The position (CEO) will reduce or maintain operation expenses within budget throughout the fiscal year." "The position (Human Resource Manager) will write recommendations to foster skill development as needed." "The position (Computer Technician) will diagnose and fix specific brand software problems daily as needed." "The position (Claims Adjuster) will process on average twenty new claims per week." "The position (Airline Attendant) will never display anger or hostility towards a rude or impolite passenger." "The position (Janitor) will clean and sanitize all lavatories daily." "The position (Supervisor) will visit and review operations at all field offices at least once per week." "The position (Customer Phone Service Representative) will answer all customer phone calls received within three rings." "The position (Public Relations Spokesperson) will file reports on activities engaged in on a daily basis." "The position (Doorman) will greet every guest with a smile." For any position, numerous statements of objectives can be written. Collectively, they are the overall job objective; individually, they represent employee accountabilities.

Conditional clauses are necessary because fulfilling job objectives is dependent on the environment, performer, and work context. Time and circumstances from within and outside the organization or worker can constrain outcomes. Why is this of particular importance in preparing the interview? It establishes the company's interest and needs while focusing the applicant's interest and desire, thus providing a template for reality testing and capability assessing within mutually apparent parameters. For example, at the completion of a position profile, it may become apparent that contractual or part-time help is a better solution than a full-time employee is. Figure 4-1 shows an abbreviated position profile for the position of Newspaper District Manager.

Figure 4-1

Position Profile
Newspaper District Manager

Objectives

1. Will use word processing, email, and proprietary computer software as needed.
2. Will contract and terminate independent contractors engaged in sales, service, and collections as needed.
3. Will use recruiting, screening, and interviewing techniques for selecting contractors as needed.
4. Will know the language of the contractor's contract and be able to explain as needed.
5. Will pick up and distribute company newspapers and material daily.
6. Will make unannounced visits days or nights to check on contractors and activities as needed.
7. Will check all customer complaints, investigate, and follow through with customers as needed.
8. Will get the factual reason(s) for all delivery stoppages and try to resell stops to minimize circulation loss as needed.
9. Will supervise and maintain accounts receivable from contractors and vendors weekly.
10. Will devise and arrange route(s) to maximize efficiency and sales as needed.
11. Will collect payments due company from contractors, vendors, subscribers, and vending machines as needed.
12. Will personally drive district route, loading and dropping off materials as needed.
13. Will supervise and train contractors and vendors as needed.
14. Will communicate by phone and in person with all contractors about service and sales weekly or as needed.
15. Will work to increase district home delivery circulation by training, coaching, and motivating contractors to solicit as needed.
16. Will verify all new sales with subscribers to see if service has begun as needed.
17. Will mediate and resolve customer and contractor disputes as needed.
18. Will canvass and solicit for single and home delivery sales opportunities as needed.
19. Will assure all district deliveries are completed by 10:00 am daily.
20. Will maintain and perform minor vending machine repairs as needed.
21. Will deposit all company monies collected into bank as needed.
22. Will submit reports and paperwork as needed.
23. Will report to Division Supervisor weekly or as needed.

Considering the above objectives as a whole, please rate yourself as to capability.

Low   1   2   3   4   5   6   7   8   9   10   High

Environmental or Specialized Work Conditions

1. Must pass physical, have valid chauffeur license, and have acceptable driving record.
2. Work begins according to schedules between 1:00 am and 4:00 am approximately.
3. ~65% of daily activities are performed outdoors in various weather conditions.
4. ~35% of daily activities are phone communication and paperwork from district office.
5. Repetitive and consistent lifting of bundles and/or materials weighing ~40 lbs.

Performance Criteria

Quarterly, written evaluations focused on district sales, service, and collection results weighted against other districts and market factors.

Crafting the Position Profile

Figure 4-1 contains four subheadings and is sequenced numerically, itemized by distinct objectives, and constructed in two similar formats. Both formats allow the interviewer and interviewee opportunities to read and discuss points with clarity from the same page simultaneously. Some organizations utilize a somewhat similar form, such as a position guide or job description. Typically, the information on these documents is condensed into paragraphs; various work activity steps are commingled and/or are written in broader and more general terms (visions). Vagueness, inadequately written work objectives, and economizing of paper diminish the effectiveness and efficiency of their use as a real tool in the selection process, as will be demonstrated. To craft a Position Profile for any job in a format similar to figure 4-1, employers should first prepare the interviewer's copy by performing the following steps.

1. Write as many statements of objectives as possible for the position.
2. Write a scale from 1 to 3, for identifying the difficulty or importance of each objective, next to each statement.
3. Using the scale in step 2 and from the employer's standpoint, mark each statement (1, 2, or 3) as to difficulty or importance.
4. Randomly arrange the statements as to difficulty or importance. Do not lump those with the same rating together.
5. Number in sequence each statement in the profile.
6. Write a scale from 0 to 6, to be used for rating an applicant's connectivity, underneath each listed statement above.
7. Include below the job objectives any noteworthy specialized conditions and performance criteria.

Prepare an identical copy for the applicant, deleting all scales except the applicant's self-rating scale. This scale should appear immediately following the objectives on the applicant's copy. The abbreviated Newspaper District Manager Profile shown in figure 4-1 would, in a completed form, serves as the applicant's copy. The last line under objectives is the applicant's self-rating scale or the degree of his or her belief in their overall job capability. Capability is not just previous job experience that is similar to the new job under consideration. It also embraces a person's range of transferable knowledge, abilities and interest that may be useful in a broad array of work situations. The (0 to 6) rating scale underneath each objective is used by the interviewer in evaluating an applicant's degree of connectivity (covert and overt factors) with the position's objectives. Number 19 below, is an example of how one statement would appear on the interviewer's longer copy for the district manager's profile.

19. Will assure all deliveries are completed by 10:00 am daily.   1   2   **3**

      Low   0   1   2   3   4   5   6   High

Evaluating the Position Profile

As will be shown later, this methodology can prove highly effective in choosing prospective employees. Also, the position profile can be modified as needed, not only to reflect job objective changes, but also as a tool for creating more objective employee performance evaluations. Further, by using commonly available application software, automated matrixes can be created which can quickly sort, collate, and compute a wide array of different results. As will be shown, using a carefully-crafted position profile over time as an interviewing tool can serve the following critical aims:

- Show employers why, how, and for what their human resources are being utilized.
- Show which candidate(s) are predicted to show strength and weakness in performing specific future work activities.
- Show where employee skill development will be most needed.
- Show what objectives are of particular importance or complexity to the organization for the position being considered.
- Provide inference to those work behaviors, both physical and mental, that would be desirable in accomplishing work activities.
- Provide an adaptable uniform rating method.
- Standardize the initial premise and structure of inquiry to each applicant.
- Provide a relevant job sketch upon which applicant and interviewer can retrieve details.
- Reduce non-verbal and verbal biases, i.e. diminish reliance on rapport.

This tool establishes a functional standard for conducting the job interview process. Standards are observable measures by which assessments are made. Yardsticks, meter sticks, bookkeeping, financials, quality control, and others represent different types of standards. They lend themselves to consistency and objectivity, whereby meaningful comparisons and judgments can be more readily determined. The position profile and scale technique is not a scientifically reliable standard, but it will provide a common basis to a business function that is highly utilized in a random way.

In looking at each objective's statement, it should be noted that no descriptive attributes of a subjective nature are included. Such adjectives as "enthusiastically," "carefully," "punctually," "trustfully," "cooperatively," "tactfully," and the like relate to a worker's deportment—conduct. The focus of the position profile is to identify facts and not abstractions. Inappropriate or inadequate employee conduct in terms of productivity, care, attendance, initiative, etc. are integral to conducting business properly, but are seldom obvious e.g. artist's portfolio or observed in the pre-employment phase. Therefore how the applicant will conduct themselves in the engagement of work activities is highly speculative and should remain an ongoing management consideration after employment.

Education, work experience, criminal background, and recent drug use checks are standard procedures for screening applicants and can protect employers against negligent hiring claims. But the fact of the matter is that those that have shown the highest propensity for the most egregious conduct in the workplace are longer-time employees and not newcomers. This should not come as a surprise to the reader, because over time, a worker's perspective customarily moves from business to social and finally personal aspects within the work environment. In time, conformity or disenchantment with a perceived group identity supersedes the intended purpose of the employee's pre-employment business expectation—to be hired to do a job. "I thought we shared (personal) common values and viewpoints (self-induced myopia). I've dedicated my life to this company. How could they (emotional trauma)?" Harsh, unpleasant, and sometimes personally devastating, but nonetheless, an event that can befall any employee. Some employees can easily lose mental clarity, falling into delusional thinking, especially given the marketing hype of the commercially-orchestrated organization as family. They forget that in the beginning, the organization didn't know and certainly didn't adopt them. All new hires should undergo a probationary period whereby management can help the new employee to understand and adopt appropriate work conduct and performance standards; otherwise, a more complicated separation may result. The lengths of probationary periods should be in direct proportion to the complexity and sensitivity of the job. Positions of higher importance should have longer probationary terms, because they supposedly impart greater value and thus pose a higher threat of disrupting organizational integrity and functioning. Unlike the interview session, evaluating employees during probation is done on the basis of genuine circumstances. Therefore, it is extremely important that management, interviewers, and new hires consider the probationary term as a critical learning period for everyone.

5
Talent and Bumps in the Dark

Talent, ability, skill, and competency are covert and overt behaviors or ways of doing something. Those involved in the employee selection process use the expression "skills are transferable" to indicate potential, aptitude, and capability. Credentials such as degrees, licenses, and certifications are evidence that particular knowledge and skills have been documented, but not necessarily acquired. If the number of applicants refused specific employment is significantly higher than those offered employment, can it be assumed that most applicants lack the proper abilities to perform? Another conclusion could be that there is a smaller number of job openings than there are applicants. Therefore, employment rejections should be more frequent—"some win, some lose." Unfortunately, attempts to validate the first assumption have been futile to date. It would require many and perhaps impossible studies whereby data is collected on the number of rejected applicants who would have been successful if they had been hired and the number of accepted applicants who later proved to be unsuccessful employees. However, U.S. Labor Department research has found that, according to surveyed employers, "Too many of today's applicants lack the needed skills to fill job vacancies, particularly in the newer, high-technology sector of the economy."

Are employee prospects ill-prepared, or are employers failing to define what skills and capabilities are really needed? In considering this question, refer back to Figure 4-1. What reading and math comprehension level does this position require? It requires a ninth-grade reading and math level equivalency, yet, the full text of the actual job description requested a bachelor's degree as a qualification. In terms of one "high tech" position, there is a common sentiment held by most workers throughout many organizations: "Be nice to the information/computer technologist, because not even the boss can make your software work." Abilities and capabilities are related, but are not the same. The gap between qualified workers and unfilled jobs in the area of high technology has much to do with judging capabilities. This is very problematic for an interviewer lacking enough knowledge regarding a specific job's high technology content.

A highly successful contract recruiter responded this way when asked if he has difficulty in finding high-tech software workers to fill jobs: "Not at all. I can fill 90% of my clients' requests relatively quickly, because I have a strong background in software. I remember, several years ago, when I began my business, I sent several qualified applicants to one company, and none were hired. But after talking with the company's boss, the reason was obvious. The boss didn't know anything about his computer needs, and each candidate was dismissed because they didn't have a degree in computer science or information technology. Computers and software have evolved beyond basic theory. Most businesses want a full-time computer technician to diagnose and fix problems, tutor their employees, and manage their computer resources and personnel. There is a huge high-tech cottage industry of hobbyist types with advanced computer-related knowledge and aptitude to accomplish those tasks, but they do not possess formal credentials. Like any other worker, some are better than others are. Remember the backyard auto mechanic? He built and repaired vehicles with a passion and obtained the required knowledge as needed. The other 10% of high-tech prospects in demand possess advanced formal education that is needed for computer-related experimental, developmental, and engineering projects. A computer is a sophisticated tool, and no more, that allows old-fashioned business stuff to be done faster, easier, and more accurately. Recruiters like me have carved out a niche by tapping auto mechanics and driving instructors. We know what, how, and where to find what 90% of the businesses that are not computer companies need."

Types of Knowledge

This type of knowledgeable recruiter is often not contracted properly by employers who seek their help to acquire highly technical employees. This subject matter expert should not only be paid a fee for finding a new employee, but he should also be compensated for conducting a job-needs assessment on the employer's behalf and delivering a position profile. Highly technical work activities are highly rule-structured and sequenced. For instance, the position profile for a Digital Satellite Technician may list the following job objective: "Will perform analysis and interpretation of digital voice and data compression algorithms using specific standards as needed." Thus, the technician does not imagine what to do, but instead performs the procedures needed. What is required is procedural knowledge, as opposed to declarative knowledge (Anderson 1987). Like driving an automobile or fixing a computer hardware problem, with practice, the steps become automatic and we can think about something else while actively performing the task. A job objective for evidencing the degree of procedural knowledge could also be written as:

Rate yourself in operating the following word processing program _____. Six means expert or the ability to instruct someone in all operations as needed.

        Low   0   1   2   3   4   5   6   High

Followed by a verbal request: "You (applicant) know how and don't know how to do what? Please explain specifically."

    Declarative knowledge, on the other hand, is more flexible and allows for more creative applications (Kintsch 1989). Principles, concepts, and facts are all varieties of declarative knowledge execution, but unlike procedural knowledge, we must consciously or actively think to use it. Thus, it has a limiting effect because it precludes other thoughts, i.e. one must concentrate. Successful work performance typically includes the interplay of both types of knowledge. Again, the position profile is a document substantiating an organization's interest. In a study of outside recruiters, it was found that employee selection aligned more with the recruiters' own work values and less with the organizations' (Adkins, Russell, and Werbel 1994). Selecting applicants for highly technical employment will require the assistance of someone with a good degree of knowledge or experience in the technical portion of the job.

Intelligence and Creativity

    Teachers, peers, and scholastic records from primary through graduate school had indicated a student as a high achiever. Once he became a professional, others thought he would rise quickly and become a recognized leader amongst his adult peers. Eleven years into his profession, his youngest brother asked him, "I'm proud of you and what you have accomplished, but do you wish you could have done more with your talents?" "I am not sure I follow you," remarked the older brother. "I mean you only got, what? Five B's in your life, and you were a star athlete in high school. You seemed destined for greatness." The older brother laughed and said, "I guess what was needed back then was clear and at hand. Things since then have not been so obvious. Besides, I'm not dead yet!" The older brother had come up short of the mark in terms of the younger brother's expectations. The older brother implied that he had achieved, but maybe needed more prompting, direction, and structure to apply his talents to other goals.

    Research studies have indicated a very weak relationship between intelligence quotient, or IQ, and success in job performance (Ghiselli 1966; Wigdor and Garner 1982). How well would a very intelligent, urban American intellectually behave and adapt if left without devices and support in a remote jungle of the Amazon? Are knowledge and experience the precursors of intelligent behavior or some innate physiological happenstance? That is the core controversy surrounding intelligence measures like IQ. Such tests are based on informational literacy and verbal reasoning. What has proven significant from research is the difficulty in differentiating the components that comprise intelligence as well as their interrelationship. General reasoning, long/short-term memory, attention span, interpreting, imagination, and problem solving are just a few of the intellectual aspects researchers are currently studying. It is, however, quite clear that being educated is not the same as being intelligent. Being educated is past tense, in that it is the attainment of specific knowledge and skills. Intellect is always an active engagement, in that it is a capacity or aptitude to use knowledge, skills, facts, relations, and so forth to learn, reason, and comprehend.

Creativity may or may not be defined as intelligence, depending on what research is accepted. Creativity is originality or an ability to make unique ideas, forms, objects, and/or interpretations. Studies to determine a relationship between creativity and intelligence (IQ scores) have shown a weak relationship if any. Studies by Amabile (1983), McCrea (1987), and Schank (1988) found personality traits of introspection, persistence, nonconformity, and curiosity of more importance than high IQ in fostering creative results. Only the last trait could possibly be evidenced in the traditional employment interview. More significantly, introspection, persistence, and nonconformity are diametrically opposed to the traditional interview's time constraints and ultimate intent—an interviewer's acceptance. This author has chosen to draw the following distinction between creativity and intelligence: As a mental process, creativity is closer to some spontaneous "unconscious insight" influenced by circumstance, whereas intelligence implies a deliberate, conscious effort to arrive at a reasonable outcome, given a situation. Imagination only becomes creativity when something tangible is made.

Thinking

> Cognition (thinking) is the process whereby an individual becomes aware or obtains knowledge of an object, a quality, or an idea.... it is possible to begin by identifying two basic cognitive or intellective modes. The one mode tends toward retaining the known, learning the predetermined, and conserving what is. The second mode tends towards revising the known, exploring the undetermined and constructing what might be. A person for whom the first mode or process is primary tends toward the usual and expected. A person for whom the second mode is primary tends towards the novel and speculative. The one favors certainty, and the other risk. Both processes are found in all persons, but in varying proportions. The issue is not of better or worse, or of useful or less useful. Both have their place, and both must be recognized for their differences, commonalties, interactions,

and distinctive functions in the individual's psychic economy. (Getzels and Jackson 1962, 14)

In attempting to gauge the future performance of an employee prospect, we reference back to the position profile. Those overt behaviors for accomplishing objectives can be accounted for by imagining or viewing those behaviors that would be displayed in the course of future work activities and writing them down. The covert behaviors are more difficult to identify. Creating, evaluating, memorizing, analyzing, reading, calculating, and organizing, among others, are mental behaviors. The strength, speed, and breadth of such abilities are as unique to an individual as are one's fingerprints or DNA. They can be value-added talents that individuals bring, sometimes becoming gold for an organization.

Interviewer: Well, we have all agreed that your credentials and qualifications are impressive. Can you shed some light on your employment interruption? You are not currently employed?

Applicant: Yeah, I was canned.

Interviewer: Hmm. Care to elaborate?

Applicant: It's none of your damn business. But since you brought it up, I wouldn't want my silence to leave you with the impression that I was in some way damaged goods. If you met my old boss in the lobby, off the record he would probably tell you that I am an arrogant, selfish, and uncooperative SOB. In short, he doesn't like me personally. So, I doubt if any recommendation will be forthcoming from him on my behalf. I would add that, off the record, we hold similar sentiments for each other. Is that clear enough for you?

Days later…

World News Headlines
Fired Unemployed Executive Picked to Head Automaker

The ways of "using one's head" are an ability and capability that an individual learns by self-instruction or independent learning. Studies on this process refer to it as cognitive strategy, executive control, productive thinking, critical thinking, and/or higher-order problem solving. A careful examination of the position profile allows recognition by interviewers of those distinct mental behaviors that could further collectively contribute to more complex performance activities. A teacher in a TV sitcom remarked, "The problem with most people is that they know all of the answers, but none of the questions. Questions, those pesky questions are the stuff of reason." An individual's critical thinking ability can be remarkably narrow or broad in scope. The wordsmith, mathematician, musician, and others can be recognized as possessing outstanding intellectual depth. Early research has shown that the intellectually gifted display exceptional versatility and a questioning curiosity (White 1931; Walberg et. al 1980). This multi-dimensional aspect of higher-order intelligence has made scientific research in this area difficult. Recent interest regarding the exceptional abilities observed in some autistic savants has moved some to believe that genius is an elemental rather than whole-brain phenomenon. Here are some abilities used in productive thinking.

- Divergent thinking: an ability to generate new or unusual ideas.

- Breaking mental sets: not being mentally rigid or seeing patterns where none exist, e.g. realizing that a hard object can be used to pound something instead of a hammer. The well-worn expression, "out-of-the-box thinking" is based on an actual test item for assessing this ability.

- Clarifying essentials: Business organizations compete for market share, not against each other.

- Avoiding premature judgments: Phone service representatives were slow in responding to customers' requests. It was thought that more training was needed. The real fix required workspace redesign for faster access to needed information.

- Attending to principles over facts: The fact that a customer is wrong is superseded by a common business principle: "The customer is always right." Therefore, an employee should avoid saying or implying to a customer that they're wrong, because a repeat business customer is always new business.

- Step-sequencing: Hill climbing, or grasping that which is obvious and firm first, but never going backward.

- Putting things together: Aspects of problem space-relatedness.

- Searching for deeper meanings: Questioning, by going beyond the obvious.

- Adaptive approaches: Degrees of readiness, i.e. "skills are transferable."
- Identifying contradictions: Being negative.
- Prioritizing: Placing elements in proper order.
- Visual imaging: Converting or translating spoken and written language to new symbols.
- Acquired knowledge execution: use all that will work.

"Models of thinking that can only deal with the world as represented in the head may find analysis of many practical thinking problems quite intractable.... Unlike formal problem solving (i.e. academic), practical problem solving cannot be understood solely in terms of problem structures and mental representations. *Practical problem solving is an open system that includes components lying outside the formal problem*—objects and information in the environment and goals and interests of the problem solver...characterized as functionally adaptive" (Scribner, S. 1986, 25-28, italics added).

Types of Reasoning

Reasoning rationally is a conscious or purposeful mental activity that draws on specific inferences from observations, facts, or assumptions. There are three distinct types of reasoning. Formal reasoning is similar to problems given to students in school. The information needed for finding a solution is present as well as the procedures or steps, and there is a single right answer. Deductive and inductive reasoning are rules of logic used in formal reasoning. Informal reasoning involves problems where there may be no single, clear answer. Furthermore, many approaches, assumptions, and solutions may be present or absent; thus, the most reasonable decision is based on what you know. Heuristics, where a course of action is suggested (e.g. a chess move) without a guarantee that the move will be correct, is one example of informal reasoning. Another example is dialectical reasoning, a process of comparing and assessing opposing points in order to arrive at a conclusion. Proposals, hiring, voting, and jury deliberations are some typical pro and con arguments which persons attempt to resolve through dialectic reasoning.

Kitchener and King did twelve years of research and found that many adults have trouble thinking dialectically. Their studies on dialectical reasoning divided it into stages of what they termed reflective judgment (critical thinking). This type of reasoning was defined as the ability to question assumptions, evaluate and integrate evidence, relate that evidence to a opinion, consider different interpretations, and reach defensible or plausible conclusions, while being willing to reassess conclusions based on new information (King and Kitchener 1994; Kitchener and King 1990). Their studies distinguished pre-reflective stages where a person's thinking is based on an inability to distinguish between knowledge and belief or between belief and evidence, and they see no reason to justify a belief. Persons at this stage assume a correct answer must exist and it can be obtained directly through one's senses (King and Kitchener 1994). "I heard the U.S. President say it." "It's common sense!" "I read it in a book." "I can read people well." These are typical thinking patterns evident in pre-reflective judgment.

In quasi-reflective stages, thinkers recognize that some things cannot be known as an absolute certainty, but they are uncertain on how to proceed in the face of uncertainty. They will defend their position by saying such things as "Based on my experience…." "We all have a right to our own opinion." According to these researchers, such defenses advance the false premises that all opinions are created equal and that knowledge is purely subjective.

Most people do not reach the reflective judgment stages until their middle or late twenties, if at all (Kitchener et al. 1993)! Persons who exhibit mature stages of reflective judgment understand that some things can never be known with certainty, yet weigh evidence in a coherent fashion towards usefulness in arriving at the best plausible conclusion or compelling understanding of an issue.

Beliefs

Resume
Mr. Low Life
666 Penitentiary Drive
Somewhere, USA

Objective:
- Seeking an executive position that uses my leadership and innovational talents.

Education:
- 11th Grade, City High School

Accomplishments:
- Built household business into an effective production and sales empire grossing over 22,000 dollars per week in less than two years.
- Managed daily cash payroll for 400 contractors and employees.
- Set up innovative software program to handle operational logistics and financial transactions.
- Devised systems of surveillance and security using high-tech equipment and personnel resources to supervise and protect business assets.

- Effective in developing public relations initiatives that served the community and business interests.
- Continually devised new and effective ways of conducting business in a highly competitive market with severe regulatory constraints.

As this illustration indicates, the main challenge in identifying productive thinking skills in employee prospects is twofold. Critical thinking is independently learned, meaning it can be developed but is not rule structured (intellect is discovery). Secondly, critical thinking is an abstract process but does not proceed from the abstract, meaning that creators and problem solvers large and small are intent on finding purposeful possibilities. According to a college professor, who had given the 'out of the box' puzzle over several years to approximately two hundred graduate students, only two of those students were ever able to find a solution. He further commented on the danger of assuming the two successful students did find the answer based solely on merit: "Another question is how important was the puzzle to the other students, considering it was a voluntary exercise to show how alternate thinking is not the norm?" Whether seeking a particular expression in art, a medical vaccine, or solutions to challenges that are more mundane, individuals must feel a personally meaningful connection to their thought. It is for these reasons that proper job interview techniques are much more critical in the evaluation of needed mental abilities.

Successfully resolving challenges generally encompasses the process of associative thinking. Based on Mr. Low Life's resume, in the absence of his past immoral and contemptible behavior, could he successfully lead an established legitimate business? Could a legitimate business executive lead Mr. Life's former criminal empire? Who would have the tougher situation? Does Mr. Low Life have the quality of reasoning (intelligence) to lead an existing legitimate business? Yes, but his problem in tackling such an endeavor is that his work would not immediately bear fruit. Mr. Low Life lacks the required associative knowledge to effectively interface and deal with normal, legal business activities at an executive level. Accepted business policies and procedures related to operations, personnel issues, financials, accounting, regulatory oversight, and so forth would require learning time on his part. Moreover, in higher job levels, employee performance becomes more orientated towards execution of emotional work and critical thinking. Although critical thinking would be in effect for either business leader, relationships (an associative factor) within a criminal enterprise are by design outside normal civility. With criminals, emotional dominance customarily supplants emotional empathy or interpersonal objectivity.

Therefore, a legitimate business executive would find it impossible even in the long term to lead Mr. Low Life's enterprise, unless he or she were comfortable with aberrant values, attitudes, motivation, and conduct appropriate to a criminal environment. In this case, that will include the use of violence and intimidation to effect power over others. The legitimate business task knowledge and skill Mr. Low Life does not possess can be realized through the comprehension of concepts and rules that are readily accessible. It is not their respective intellectual ability but their readiness to take some action(s) in the light of a situation that would determine success.

How can interviewers more effectively gauge an applicant's thinking skills for positions requiring a preponderance of judgmental activities? In business, thought and knowledge from diverse areas (personnel, management, technology, processes, evaluation, etc.) and complexity may be utilized in facing challenges. Is thinking a subset of objective knowledge? If so, then no infant would be able learn to think, and our imaginations would not be possible—or, as one writer remarked, "If children had adult power to execute actions, then may God save us all." As shown, the ability to execute critical thinking is different than decision-making. The former is a mental activity, and the latter is a belief. A few years ago, the American medical profession dismissed acupuncture as unscientific hocus-pocus, and today some medical schools offer training in its application. Most often, we adopt a mental stance on the basis of intellectual subjectivity or emotional comfort with little regard as to why it is reasonably justifiable. What we hold to be true can affect our perceptions and interpretations. Thinking critically or associatively requires a concerted effort, and it is not a mental reflex or passing notion. Job interviewing is a processing tool for predicting the best employee choice. It must, therefore, be based on job-related facts and not personal suppositions. This helps in avoiding not only the emotional, but also intellectual, traps that limit our adaptability in comprehending those realities (strangers) that we are unaccustomed to.

The position profile is a tangible bridge to connect an applicant's capabilities to perform or accomplish work activity objectives. Demonstrating associative thinking abilities using the position profile is based on the word-association tests which behavioral scientists use in evaluating verbal creativity. Wallach and Kogan (1965) suggested "that if we arrange a situation in such a manner that only appropriate associations are provided by the individual, greater creativity should be indicated by the ability to produce more associations and to produce more that are unique" (14). Those authors have also noted that ample time must be allowed for responses. The position profile must be provided to the job applicant before the interview to provide them ample time to review and think.

6
Applicant Beware

Not all interviewers are equal to their task! They may be new and/or lack the proper training, resources, and personal motivation to execute a job interview properly. Their boss may have given them a special assignment, such as "Hire a person who does not exceed five feet in height." Unless you fit that stature, you will not be considered for the job. There are three things applicants must concern themselves with before engaging in the traditional interview. Number one is purely arbitrary, but unfortunately the most critical:

1) projected image
2) skills
3) motivation

Projected Image

Your image, in part, is characterized by physical appearance: facial looks, physique, diction, hygiene, gestures, manners, and attire. For the purposes of interviewing, it is the image you project and how it is perceived by another, and not your interpretation of how you seem, that is important. Many people find the smell of cigarette smoke or fragrances on a person to be highly offensive. Interviewees would therefore be wise to have interview apparel cleaned and be free of distinctive odors before the meeting. Much has been written on the importance of good grooming and dress in meeting would-be employers. Tacky dress can be more effective than tasteful dress in conveying positive impressions. For example, at a job fair two young recruiters amused themselves by distinguishing those who were accustomed to giving orders from those who took orders. The well-dressed individuals in the crowd were considered boss types. Now, imagine if an impeccably-dressed applicant who was applying for a team player position (diffused authority) had come to their booth and dropped off a resume. Would these recruiters presume this applicant to be too aloof to fit the team? Don't team players all wear the same uniform? Prejudice does not only extend to dress; mannerisms can affect projected image too. Regional sales managers dismissed prospects from further employment consideration for not being animated enough, meaning those applicants did not display "strong vibes"—failed to fidget in chairs and/or showed few hand gestures. This was interpreted as a lack of energy, boldness, or dynamism. Oddly, the two sales managers were very conservative and reserved in their own mannerisms.

Finding the Image

What's an applicant to do in order to project a more favorable image? An individual must imagine seeing through the eyes of a total stranger (the interviewer). One must become an actor/actress. What is the proper stage costume to be in character? Books, magazines, television, movies, and actual observation can help in locating a successful appearance. Researching media and actual observations may afford glimpses of mannerisms and speech to model. You are acting a part for an unknown critic, and you want a good review. He or she is not interested in seeing your substance. What is needed is a terrific stage performance. Overcome stage fright by rehearsing appropriate responses to anticipated questions. Materials on types of questions you may be asked, with appropriate replies, appear abundantly in print media and on the internet. This is not sarcasm or whimsy; individuals pay hundreds and thousands of dollars to firms so that they can be transformed into a more marketable image. Recall, first impressions typically are biases forming categories of significant weight. Your substance (abilities and motivation) as a potential contributor to the organization's future accomplishments is secondary in the image-type interview.

As an applicant, if you are to be competently interviewed, it is your job to promote your abilities, capabilities, and motivation to perform the work. As mentioned, you should have a position profile, or at least a job description, to review before the face-to-face. If one is not offered during appointment scheduling, then inquire about it. Suppose the company informs you that such documentation will not be available. Then you are definitely stepping into the image-type interview. Your resume/application and interview presentation will be used to vaguely predict future job fit. This method is a total disadvantage to the organization, unless the company is interviewing to select a "hard closer" or a verbally persuasive employee. If that is the case, the image interview offers the best opportunity for a company to select candidates who may be immediately successful at persuasiveness. For all other types of applicants, including wannabe salespersons, the image interview can be an uncontrollable blessing or disaster.

The interviewer uses your script (resume/application) or theirs to critique your interview performance. Yet it must be presumed that, while listening to and watching you, they have already cast you for an imaginary part about which you know little. You are improvising a fictional character (job title), a character without defined substance that will act in a play that has no storyline. What should you do? Build your own themes around the job title. Create a fictional script around the job title and deliver it by asking lead questions to build further. "What are some of the things you want me to do? How many employees will be working in my department? Do they do the same things I will be doing? Can you tell me about some of the critical challenges or problems that may have arisen in the past?" You can build an imaginary story, but if your mind does not lend itself to fiction—if you are not a good storyteller and are unable to provide quick responses—the curtain may fall prematurely. You are obliged to be interesting and entertaining without an element of drama. Missed lines, dead space, and deep analysis will not make you a hit, no matter how competent you are in areas that are more job-critical. You are a visual sound bite, not any different than a product advertised on television—it is the audience's impression that counts. Soap comes scented or unscented, but it's all soap!

In the words of the late entertainer George Burns, "The secret to being a good actor is honesty. If you can fake that, you've got it made." So you are acting well, the stage is yours, and suddenly the interviewer presents a question and expects a concrete reply. "How do you motivate?" He asks.

Your options:

1. Say, "I can't explain it. I just do it." Should the interviewer take this to mean sincerity? Has he posed a procedure or concept?

2. Define motivation, which does not answer this procedural question.

3. Ask for specific situational example. This could be dangerous; it requires the interviewer to think. He wasn't prepared in the first place, and now you want him to be creative. Situational examples typically are not detailed or broad enough, being bound by the limits of information provided. This can create a problem for a person who can really think. They tend to consider the obvious and more. But, you are not selling your concept of motivation; therefore, only a reply that is acceptable is warranted.

4. Say, "I am not sure what you mean." The interviewer can infer that to mean many things. "It was a simple question; is the applicant implying I asked a dumb question?" Or, "It should have been clear in the first place. Is the applicant not listening or dense?"

5. "Well, I have used coaching in the past, among other techniques." This would be an acceptable reply.

When asked to answer vague or open-ended questions such as this, keep your response short but acceptable. Acceptable responses are not the best or the worst replies, but they are always safe. "How I motivate depends on many factors and the circumstances. I am not sure how you want me to respond." This would be a more intelligent reply, but the interviewer may know very little about motivational procedures or may not be particularly interested in the subject. Also, keep in mind that some interviewers indulge in "'mind games." "What can I do for you?" asks the interviewer in a surly tone to the applicant sitting for his or her appointment. "Offer me employment," replies the befuddled applicant. "Why should I do that?" retorts the interviewer. Such a provocation may be offered to see how the person may react, whereby the applicant's assertiveness or passivity is supposedly assessed, i.e. risk-taking, instead of coming to the point and saying to an applicant, "Would being verbally manipulative, confrontational, or argumentative to win purely for the sake of winning be to uncomfortable for you to handle? Have you ever done that?" Or such off-handed speech on the part of the interviewer could be due to simplemindedness or an ego trip. In a journal article, it was reported that a group of seasoned interviewers individually made hiring determinations before the interview had been in progress five minutes (Tullar et.al. 1974)! In such circumstances, the job interview is merely perfunctory. Winning a mind game may mean losing the prize. The best advice: do not show your emotions in a business situation. Taking the opportunity to step out of your acting role through the real use of your intellect, discernment, or judgment can be liberating, but fatal. Will intelligent responses make an interviewer feel defensive or uncomfortable? Should you risk making an unfavorable impression? How motivated are you in to have that job? Such questions are personal assessments.

Motivation

One's motivation is of paramount importance. In fact, it is the driving force of human effort. An individual can have boundless talent and perform poorly because proper motivation to do the best one can do is absent. Most employers desire highly-motivated workers more than skilled workers. They can teach many skills, but not desire. Motivation has been described as a need and drive—the "why" of behavior. People who are thirsty or hungry are driven to drink or eat. This is easily understood in a physiological way, but in most other ways, one's motivation to want to do something (a quality job) is a voluntary choice. In 1921, Stanford University began an ongoing study wherein subjects with the top one percent in childhood IQ scores were tracked throughout their lives. Some of the gifted failed to live up to their early intellectual promise, dropping out of school or drifting into intellectually low-level work. Decades later, when the university compared 100 of the most successful subjects with 100 of the least successful, they found motivation had made the difference (Terman and Oden 1959).

An employee's motivation and abilities determine the quality of work performance. Interviewers cannot determine if an applicant will be a really motivated employee in terms of future work for the same reasons as outlined for personality typing. However, it is part and parcel of the image in their heads. Autonomy, compensation, prestige, benefits, authority, skill development, and job activity are some inducements that organizations can offer their employees as work incentives. In return, employees are expected to provide work performances that at some point fulfill an organization's need and drive. Examining inducements that an organization offers can provide valuable clues to applicants in projecting the "correct" motivational image.

Employment Motivators

Organizational Inducements (Motivators)	**Applicant Motivation**
Recognition (achieved or allocated)	Distinction
Authority (allocated)	Power
Empowerment (allocated)	Autonomy
Skill Development (allocated or achieved)	Betterment
Benefits (allocated)	Bargains
Compensation (allocated or achieved)	Income
Job (allocated)	Job Interest

The job aspect is a given if the applicant has received an invitation to interview. Whether seeking employment in the lower ranks or the uppermost levels of an organization, an applicant's interest is evident. Will the interviewer find it reasonable, convincing, and focused on the job? Keep in mind, once employed, meeting the employer's work standards is crucial. Handling customer phone inquiries may seem simplistic, but one's use of tact, diction, comprehension, memory, feedback, and knowledge distinguishes such activity from the ordinary. If an applicant's projected image does not fit the interviewer's understanding of what's important, they won't have luck.

Frequently the interviewee is eliminated at this juncture, not because they lack appropriate skills to do the job, but because they are educationally or experientially overqualified. "I've been a successful executive for over ten years and hold two advanced degrees. Now, I want to wash dishes for a living. Can I do that for you?" That no one can be over-qualified for a particular job is true. The questionable logic that is typically given for dismissing such applicants is that they will not be satisfied with their job duties because the job will be too mundane to hold their interest. The over-qualified will quit sooner than someone with lesser qualifications would. Research supports this contention.

The fact that the over-qualified applicant has a greater potential of bringing added value immediately is dismissed in favor of lesser qualifications for a position requiring lesser ability. In other words, today's bargain is put off for tomorrow's pittance. Although there are many studies focusing on the lack of job contentment amongst the "over-qualified," there is an absence of research on what constitutes a positive relationship between an employee's ability to perform at various levels and job contentment in determining employee retention. Do those employed in more menial jobs leave at questionably higher rates due to job tasks or other reasons (working conditions, pay, opportunity, etc.) in comparison to those employed in more enriched jobs? Would a rent-a-cop making twenty dollars per hour give more longevity than another one making seven dollars per hour, given both have the same background? Are prophetic yearnings to foretell another's fate rational in light of our own uncertain futures? It would seem that if a job has to be done, it would surely need attending to sooner rather than later. A need to fill a job, therefore, would seem a more tenable concern for the employer than the uncertainty.

Finding someone to do the basic work is much easier than finding someone that can add additional value to an organization at the same price. Maybe the executive is seeking a less stressful life situation or needs more time for writing her memoirs? Today in the U.S., "one employer for life" is no longer a proposition any reasonable employer would offer or employee should view as a guarantee. Therefore, as an applicant, if you are rejected for employment on the basis of being over-qualified, you should make further inquiries to determine the real reason(s).

For arcane reasons, raising the question of compensation by an applicant is generally considered taboo during the interview. However, organizations should tell an applicant the minimum compensation they are prepared to pay for a position at the start of the interview. This is not advocating an offer of employment or negating the possibility of negotiations once an offer is made. How is an applicant to be motivated when the most typical and major information sought by applicants cannot be realistically considered (Barber and Roehling 1993)? Added incentives like stock options, bonus sharing, MBO's, gain sharing, and so forth, if applicable, should also be mentioned without detailing particulars.

As a rule, most private organizations, unlike governmental ones, do not divulge even minimum pay prior to the interview discussion. Some employers go further, heaping personal insult upon individuals in this regard by requiring applicants to provide salary histories when applying. So, don't be shocked if you are pressed to give an income you would like to earn during an interview session. A pat response could be: "I am sure you will be fair. So whatever you would pay your best candidate is an amount I would consider." On the other hand, if a prospect is confident that they bring to the table unique or highly sought after talents, then the hard money game should be played to the hilt.

Here are a few considerations that applicants should address before attempting to negotiate compensation:

- After receiving a verbal/written employment offer with proposed salary, be sure to thank the prospective employer. Then inform him/her that you would like to think about the offer overnight. Don't forget to ask the hiring person what would be a good time for you to get back to them with your decision.

- How many employees will be occupying the same position? More workers holding identical positions typically indicate less negotiating power, processing jobs being a prime example. The employer has offered the position based on the premise that applicant will be able to meet well-defined or procedural work behaviors in meeting job objectives. Assuming the labor pool has an ample supply of desired workers, there is little incentive for the employer to consider paying a higher hiring salary for work already being accomplished at a lower rate by others. Solitary or fewer identical positions are more indicative of a position where an applicant will have more discretion in applying his/her abilities, because the employer is dependent on fewer workers to fulfill the position's responsibilities. In the former case, the outstanding performer can demonstrate their work superiority over comparable employees once on board. Those hired for positions that are more solitary may have talents and experience making them more attractive to the employer than other applicants, but they must offer convincing explanations as to why.

- Are your talents and experience noteworthy and unique? How do you know?

- Has the applicant researched reliable sources to know the pay range offered for similar positions and organizations situated in the same region?

- What will be your approximate monthly out-of-pocket cost of living expenses? Lease, mortgage, dependents, neighborhood, food, gas, loans, utilities, clothes, savings, taxes, entertainment, etc. One- or two-income household? U.S. government statistics defined poverty to be income of approximately $15,000 per year or less for a family of three! As stated in the introduction, those who are more financially secure have a different employment perspective. Your prospective employer may be uninformed as to life's current economic realities. Educate him with facts.

- Will you be willing to compromise on salary, and if so, by what amount?
- Don't leave your current job until a final new job offer is received in writing, and do not be afraid to ask for an offer in writing.

Benefits are those organizational initiatives and programs that can improve the quality of life for employees. They represent and are a part of an employee's total compensation package. They are not provided because the employer wants to be a benefactor; rather, they represent a sound business strategy by the organization to attract and retain employees from the available labor market. In addition, upper management and principals can reduce their own living expenses by spreading such costs over the organization's total workforce. Health insurance, dental insurance, retirement plans, paid training, fitness centers, clubs, flex time, perks, and so forth are value-added aspects of an employment situation. As an applicant, you may be interested in particular "bennies." Also, you may choose to opt out of some customary employer-provided benefits, but will the employer then pay you that deferred cost?

Employee skill development is a necessary process used by organizations to improve operational effectiveness and efficiency. As its future operators, job applicants must have willingness and the prerequisite skills to continually learn new information and skills. This has become an imperative, stemming from our new information economy, globalization, and the high frequency of technological change.

Empowerment is an organizational principle whereby employees are granted more input in administrating a business's activities. "Can it be done better? Let us know how." Herein lies the greatest danger for the applicant with productive thinking skills. The image interview promotes mediocrity. The "using of one's head" is a personal ability. Applicants that wish to use their heads must avoid the appearance of arrogance, especially if the interviewer could be the prospect's boss. Aside from the top leader, the most autonomous positions in most large, privately-run organizations are those of janitor, interviewer, and, most recently, computer/information technologist.

Positions of authority where one has considerable influence over ideas, things, and/or persons can be a troubling notion, because authority and leadership are not the same. Authority is a label that identifies someone as holding the power to influence or make decisions. Leadership is an ability to influence something that is "voluntarily" recognized or accepted by others as a demonstrated claim to that "something's" ownership. One could be a physician and have authority under state license to dispense medicine, or one could be a physician and be a leader in one's field by finding a cure for a disease. Another leader could be a claims adjuster whose knowledge and abilities, customer satisfaction, or productivity ratings make superiors and co-workers gravitate to him or her for guidance. Such outstanding employees become de facto leaders without the allocated label of "authority figure."

Within the military, leadership and authority are never given separate distinction, except after the heat of direct battle in which special acts were done. It must have an absolute command authority hierarchy to direct all elements it controls as a single power. Although encouraging voluntary leadership would be very desirable from a business perspective, in the military, this would undermine discipline and slow responsiveness, thus diminishing its efficiency and effectiveness in dealing with crisis.

Authority needs others to have an identity, whereas leadership is a projection of self that others can identify with. As an old adage warns, "The Devil, though suspect, has led many to hell." Obviously, persons of questionable character and intellect can effectively lead others. Simply having someone believe that there is benefit in following or accepting can carry the moment or a longer recognition of leadership. Applicants vying for authority roles should model the attitudinal and behavioral attributes of effective leadership within the context of business. The following are representative of some:

INTEGRITY	OUTCOMES	PRACTICALITY	RESOURCEFULNESS
OBJECTIVITY	VISION	AWARENESS	COMPREHENSION
DECISIVENESS	CLARITY	OPTIMISM	FALLIBILITY

MULTI-DIRECTIONAL SENSITIVITY (SUPERIORS-SUBORDINATES-OTHERS)

The desire for recognition or distinction is a normal tendency. Promotions, awards, bonuses, and so forth are special favors that organizations give. Some workers curry favor through pandering and some through personal performance. If an applicant is ambitious for advancement, personal motives must be framed in the context of work performance. "As I progress with the company and develop, would there be other opportunities I could explore in the future?" This imparts several distinct impressions to the interviewer: a) the prospect is career-focused, not just job-focused; b) the applicant is willing to develop; and c) the candidate is adaptable to change. Those are favorable hiring images without the clarity of more objective predictability factors. Old-fashioned "brown-nosing," or pandering, is becoming harder to exercise because, as mentioned in a previous chapter, "information's discretionary reach" is ever-increasing in the work place. Authority itself is less secure and much more subject to performance scrutiny than in the past. Waters that superiors must navigate are further from shore, choppier, and much deeper to manage. Astute business authorities are concerned with keeping their operations moving. This requires more than a pleasant breeze on the backside.

Harsh Realities

As stated, stepping out of an acting debut through the real use of intellect, discernment, or judgment can be liberating, but fatal. How motivated are you in wanting a particular employment situation? Each job candidate must know his or her abilities and motivations. Furthermore, how do those characteristics relate to expected job activities and the organization's motivators? Allocated motivators are generally not as plentiful, thereby more difficult to obtain. An applicant's ambition for these must be tempered with shrewdness. Does a prospective boss want more of a personal ally, personal servant, general worker, or leader? One's presentation, or how one displays various kinds of 'smart' behaviors—when to be flippant or serious or when to stay task-focused, thus perhaps putting a social relationship at risk—are some of the types of intelligence others may expect (Goffman 1959; Covington and Omelich 1979).

For instance, you are an experienced machinist. Your new boss, an engineer, tells you to make a hollow pipe out of a rectangular piece of stock. Based on your know-how, you decide it is better to bore the hole first, and then afterward shape the outside. He orders you to do the opposite. Argue to do the job right as you see it, or please the boss? The overriding principle in the conduct of business should be quality performance. A superior's directive or optimizing a business performance can be an awkward affair. You tell the engineer "Okay," but then do it your way. Later, the engineer comes to you and examines the hollow pipe, and then asks you some questions. To your astonishment, he was not interested in making a hollow pipe, but was experimenting with materials. Consequently, the last question should undoubtedly beg the employee's indulgence and is a concern for the job-seeker only after the curtain falls.

One's level of desire for self-validation, what one thinks and feels is important to oneself before or during employment can cause serious personal frustration for the following reason. Applicants and workers fail to recognize the difference between being employed and being self-employed. The former is a bilateral agreement obligated under external control, whereas the latter is personal autonomy obliged to external agreement. Organizations, however, have been quick to perpetuate the myth of a family circle, thus adding to an employee's possible confusion. Employment, at its core, remains a condition of economic utility. It must always be remembered that no organization is obliged to validate a worker's idealized self. If a person identifies who they are too closely with their role as an employee, then by definition "the self" will be compromised, because it now requires external justification to realize internal merit. What one person deems important may or may not be important to another.

7
Applicant Controls

It can be quite an inconvenience to run out of gas, downright embarrassing when we take a passenger along for the ride. "My gas gauge is broken. I thought I had enough to take us further." Before embarking on a job interview, an applicant must know where they're headed and that their fuel tank of knowledge and abilities is full. They will need enough fuel for at least a sixty-minute drive in stop-and-go traffic. Another little tip from those that have driven this course before is that high-octane fuel (more refined) costs more but can burn longer and cleaner than low-octane.

Picking Destination(s)

Management	Finance/Accounting	Sales	Marketing	Research
Clerical	Executive	Personnel	Technology	Advertising
Labor	Crafts	Service	Training	Support

Doing the work that one thinks he/she wants to do is more than a notion. Doing the work that someone else is paying for can be more than a nuisance. Ask a book editor. Typically, we don't look beyond our individual abilities, motivations, and interests when considering employment. We imagine what the positive personal aspects will be, yet consider little of others' demands that may be placed upon us in fulfilling a position. A successful young physician remarked, "I spent most of my life pursuing and establishing my medical practice. It was my dream and passion. Now the routine and the reality of the profession have caused me to forget what that dream really was. I had never imagined the hospitals, the group administration, the risks, the pressures, the cost, and my family in my picture." When asked, "Would you have chosen something different if you had known the real picture?" he answered, "No. Because I am not expressing regret in choosing as I chose. I am confessing my astonishment at my earlier innocence and conceit. It was only I in my picture." As an organizational employee, a person is more likely to have less work freedom than this doctor.

Mapping Terrain

Bureaucratic   Manufacturing   High Tech.   Service   Multi-Faceted
Large   Office/Field   Union   New   Mature

Those physical and social interactions (job context) that directly impact your job can influence your thoughts, abilities, and attitudes about the job beyond the requirements of job content (what's done and how). Smaller and newer companies offer less anonymity and therefore greater opportunity to expand your job content. However, since closer familiarity among all employees is also more likely, there is more pressure towards conformity, particularly in terms of an expected group identity.

Blue-collar jobs like mining, construction, policing, and other such physically demanding and potentially dangerous jobs require a mental toughness to augment physical strength and body endurance. It is not surprising that many workers so employed tend to communicate with harshness and profanity (shop talk). Such expressive patterns may serve as a coping mechanism by diminishing emotional passivity and keeping them pumped for action. Newcomers entering such ranks may have to be prepared to steel themselves also. Failing to do so may make veteran workers perceive the newcomer as unable to carry their share of a burden (mental stress) for the distance. On the other hand, some employees may find such language so personally uncomfortable that they believe the work environment to be a hostile one. "Psyching" is a culturally-learned coping mechanism for channeling internal energy to maintain a mental posture for enhancing physical action under direct duress. Similarities between these employment settings and the military or sports arena are not just coincidental.

Bureaucratic organizations are almost extinct in the private business sector, but they remain the predominant structure in governmental organizations, representing the biggest and most complex business organizations as well as collectively the largest employer in the nation. Elected officials establish public policy, influence public attitude, and broker power. They have few but heavy responsibilities and are immediately accountable only to each other. It is wishful or naïve thinking, given the magnitude and assortment of individual private interests, for elected officials to serve all the people. The concept of enacting blind or impartial justice in their decision-making is more a fettered than free one, honor and integrity to ideals being suppressed under the weight of personal ambition and commitments to significant others. The practical consideration of showing integrity by honoring those who have been or can be of greater personal assistance diminishes objectivity. This premise poses the major dilemma to critical thought, and therefore decision-making, in our governments.

Persons through their money and votes are purchasing power and influence, and not an elected official's ability to reason or make good decisions on behalf of the public. This is why candidates campaigning for elected positions are constantly peppered with questions about what they said or did in the past. Their responses imply to what degree they value adaptability over reliability. Elected officials are products and not resources; therefore, they are expected to be immutable in terms of utility and not transformable. Political purchasers and investors consider expressing a change in one's opinion on the basis of a better understanding of facts and information a risky proposition. Governments in America, by design and procedure, give priority to businesses opportunities for personal gain(s) over public service or the realm of objectivity. Thus, the most vital job skill needed by the elected is being able to deflect criticism and present non-substantive or neutral rhetoric that cannot be easily challenged (visions). Those trained as lawyers seem to do this best, and occupy most elected positions or serve as senior staffers to such power brokers.

Civil servants or non-political employees manage, research, analyze, craft the policies, and provide the procedural know-how and so forth whereby governments perform public service functions. Due to stringent civil service testing and score rankings used in many governmental job classifications, as a hired group, they are above average in terms of measured competencies. It is not surprising that these workers seldom, if ever, are encouraged or allowed to address the public. Between their varied assessments and opinions is where the effectiveness of government can be found. Unlike the elected and their chosen staff, civil servants are typical organizational employees. Unfortunately, there seems to be a common public perception that as a whole, government workers are lazy and unproductive. This erroneous assumption has more to do with the nature of government itself and its purpose than with group work behaviors. Civil servants themselves seem to have a group perception towards the elected and their staff that is much more disdainful than that found among workers in similar subordinate positions found outside government. They view the elected as caricatures because there's no regular cycle of observable and tangible products or services of major public impact that the elected must deliver. Other than typical speeches and approvals, major policy initiatives are rare at any level of government. Therefore, civil servants maintain and have ultimate operational control, leaving the elected without much daily purpose in their eyes—government is the people's. In contrast, the private business leader is the business; success or failure has a face.

Government is the largest most diversified employer in America, controlling an absolute non-competitive market, and is supposedly fiduciary in purpose. Special attention or service priority, like in any other business, is provided to customers deemed most important. Unlike other businesses, governments do not offer tailored products or services as a rule. Therefore, the only customer option that can be had from government is special delivery. Whether a city, state, or the federal government, the demand to be serviced, in the eyes of citizens or the civil servant, should not be based on privilege. Yet, with every expedited exception that is granted from on high, work productivity becomes less important while work demand continues. The elected officials and their emissaries are focused on the top priorities of brokering policy and power; they rely on civil servants to run the government. As an elected official once admonished, "In this environment, we only note our successes because appearance is what counts at the end of the day." This prevailing attitude is cascaded downward from the elected to appointees and finally the civil employee, emphasizing position preservation over consistency in customer service and productivity. From their beginnings, governmental entities have had no market competitors, and have had automatic revenue in terms of taxes and fees. With no profit motive and no need for customer loyalty—where else can they go?—the appearance of competence becomes the performance measure.

This has in the past made it a haven for employment nesting or featherbedding, whereby the performance of highly productive as well as incompetent employees is easily obscured, impeding the need for positive and innovative changes in functionality and development from within government. The vast majority of citizens or government owners has little accessibility to the particulars behind actions and inaction and can exert attention to needs most effectively through group power and wealth. But there are hundreds and even thousands of groups, not to mention the solitary citizen, seeking such attention. This leaves less quality and urgency for many changes. When an irate citizen called a radio show and began blasting her elected representative for alleged failures, the host snapped back, "You're not the only one that votes and pays taxes, so let's be civil." Deflecting responsibility and accountability is easy when there are so many bosses running the business at so many levels. So whether sincere and competent or neither, nesting provides cover for governmental workers from the highest to lowest levels until some event manages to penetrate its many insulating twigs.

Gradually whistle-blowers, computers, and cost/benefit analyses are penetrating work and performances within government institutions, while privatization and comprehensive investigative reporting by media are making leaders and workers subject to deeper assessments. Baltimore, Maryland, became the first municipality in the nation to implement a formal, nonpolitical system of accountability and evaluation for its various departmental administrations and public service functions. The results and reviews in the first couple of years were so outstanding that staffs from other cities throughout the nation and abroad have traveled there to learn.

To work in a governmental bureaucracy, whether at the federal or local level, is unique in a number of ways. The pace of government work is typically slower and compensation is below comparable private sector jobs, but the chance for longer-term security is better. Singular career advancement based on performance merit is slow and will continue to be so, because team play and management/labor agreements are more important than innovation or results in government work. Government offers a wide array of different work settings. Some employees make a career of changing jobs without ever leaving their government employer.

It is interesting to note that labor unions developed as a direct result of an early bureaucratic business practice, i.e. arbitrary, unaccountable power. Everyone in the U.S., employed or retired, owes, in great part, their overall employment or retirement compensation to the labor movement, irrespective of whether they were ever a part of a union or not. "A fair day's wage for a fair day's work" is a union slogan. It gave rise to the concept of market pricing, where the amount and type of employee compensation is formulated based on an industry standard. Unionism contributed directly and indirectly to consumers (employees) by the rippling effect of its compensation policies across major industries and occupations, thereby benefiting producers (employers) also. More compensation to consumers meant more spending by consumers, which in turn meant more revenue for producers. Although collective bargaining equalizes compensation and benefits across a group, this union practice also inhibits an individual member's opportunity for singular merit gain. A labor union's purpose for existence and earnings are based on the protection of its members' interest. Similarly, political parties and legislative bodies are effectively organized labor unions. Unions can hinder or assist an employer's particular agenda. There are many other examples that relate to a job's context. Considering as many of them as possible before choosing a particular employment situation should make adjusting to a new job easier.

Organizational climate can be a surprising employment property. Managers and supervisors are a workplace's strongest currents. A late-night weather report tells you that rain is expected tomorrow. So in the morning on the way out, you grab your rain gear, and then it doesn't rain all day. If you hadn't heard the weather report, would you have prepared the same way? Regardless of the interviewer's opinion of the climate surrounding your prospective employment, be prepared to handle changing climates without notice. This caution is particularly important for younger job applicants and employees. As mentioned earlier, research has shown they are not able to read non-verbal communication as well as older persons. Then again, perhaps the younger workers are a bit more idealistic and less constrained by the chains of material independence—"Hello parents, I'm back."

Higher Octane Fuel

| Specialized Courses/Training | Certificates | Licenses | Accomplishments | Awards |

Lower Octane Fuel

Problem Solving	Arranging	Calculating	Examining	Evaluating
Persuading	Planning	Recording	Improving	Bookkeeping
Creating	Organizing	Clarifying	Delegating	Presenting
Diagnosing	Extrapolating	Synthesizing	Writing	Purchasing
Collecting	Supervising	Leading	Counseling	Motivating
Researching	Monitoring	Defining	Reading	Designing
Conversing	Explaining	Editing	Using tools	Statistics
Formulating	Verifying	Operating	Computing	Instructing
Coordinating	Prospecting	Inspecting	Promoting	Assembling
Sorting	Coaching	Acting	Dexterity	Specifying
Conducting	Filing	Selling	Closing	Muscle

It is important for an applicant to frame his skills in the proper context—business. Qualifications, skills, and capabilities are an individual's stock for trade. Although the image interview seldom examines the tangible values an applicant may offer, it is imperative that an applicant is able to express them when needed. But you should not express your skills merely as word action verbs. "I can organize and do research" does not have the same texture and strength as "I've spent a lot of time researching and organizing financial data from manual file records and computer databases" or "I am not intimidated easily; therefore, I would have little problem in supervising difficult workers."

The Occupational Outlook Handbook published by the U.S. Government has over two hundred and fifty unique occupational listings with associated descriptions of work activities, and is available at most libraries. By designing and studying a personal interest and skill matrix similar to the one above, an applicant can develop significant knowledge of their interest, abilities and capabilities. It is not the prospective employer's business to define your interest. "Can you do the job?" and "Why should I choose you?" should be their only considerations. As a job-seeker, the better you know your abilities, your motivations, and the interview concept, the better will be your chances of landing that job you want.

In concluding the interview, the interviewer should ask an applicant "Do you have any questions or comments?" Applicants may use this opportunity to ask pertinent business questions that may be important to them. But it is essential that an applicant include the following response: "Yes. I am very interested in securing this job. I am confident in my abilities and capabilities to perform. What is your impression of me as an applicant, and how soon will a decision be made?" If the interviewer replies positively, then you may be selected. But if the interviewer replies negatively or ambiguously, then you must ask him/her to share their concerns for the sake of business clarity. Unless an applicant believes they lack the ability to perform the job or has no interest in a particular position, the interviewee must close on a desirable note. Always remember that although you may be qualified, others may present more and better-refined qualifications.

Know Business's Intent

Fortunately, if you are provided a position profile prior to the job interview, it can be a significant help as a road map. By planning your interview trip ahead of time, you can anticipate the obvious, thus save time and fuel. Moreover, when a prospective employer gives you a position profile, it is a special invitation that says, "This is not a mystery tour. We are seriously considering your services to fulfill our needs. Are you interested and able to help us at this time? If so, travel to see us, but we suggest you give some thought to, be prepared to see some sights and be an active participant in some activities if you decide to stay awhile."

People call on strangers to come into their homes and lives all the time to provide personal services and products. After the service has been performed, the customer may remark in disgust, "If I had only known, I would have chosen someone else." The prospective employer is the applicant's prospective customer, and the profile is a list of objectives(s) the customer needs to have done by someone. Employment is your business service and not the employers', unless the employer is in the business of providing employment services. To be unemployed does not mean one is unable to do business; it means one has no customer to do business with. What, then, distinguishes the self-employed from the organizational employee? The self-employed have high self-confidence in their ability to acquire their work resources (money, material, persons, etc), as well as attract and keep customers to the degree necessary for generating enough profit for themselves. This mindset is not semantics; it represents a core difference in employment perspective.

In the late seventies, a New Yorker's story became national news. A stockbroker in his forties lost his job of many years. Since he was married and the sole provider for his family, indebtedness made maintaining an adequate income a desperate situation. For a long time, his family never knew that he had lost his stock brokerage job, because each morning after losing his job, he continued to go to work, earning enough in tax-free income to manage his accustomed living expenses. No longer the unemployed, instead he became self-employed with a new job title—beggar. He took the subway to the train station every morning, went to a locker, exchanged his business suit for well-worn apparel, and then proceeded to some pedestrian promenade to panhandle. This man did not view organizational employment or type of job as a personal entitlement or important to his self-concept. His focus was finding customers so that he could derive an income. He found and serviced a conscious interest of individuals--charity.

Therefore, when an applicant receives a solicited position profile to review prior to the job interview, one must consider the business proposition with the utmost importance and discernment. News reporters are taught to use the "5W and H" query method to gather information: "What? Who? Why? Where? When? and How?" A carefully crafted position profile answers many of those questions beforehand. As an applicant, you are being asked to explore further those answers (objectives) provided in the profile in order to convince your prospective customer (employer) of the extent to which you are ready, willing, and able to perform the need (job) as outlined. The "How?" and "Why?" should be the foremost questions you should consider for each objective, because unlike the other four "Ws," these two lean mostly towards opinion and not fact. For example:

> How do I get my work?
> Do I solicit it?
> Given to me by whom (customers/co-workers)?
> Paper or computerized retrieval system?
> How is my work important?
> How does it fit in?
> Is it process, regulatory, emotional, political, and/or innovative?
> Why is my work important?
> Policymaking, procedural, and/or policy executing?
> Does it relate to time, revenue, quantity, and/or quality?
> What software programs may be helpful and how?
> What has to be done before an intended outcome is realized?
> Do I manage/supervise personnel, processes, paper, and/or policies?
> What should my productivity be, quality- and/or quantity-wise?
> Do I have to discover, persuade, memorize, compile, initiate, and/or create?
> What must I be able and ready to do my first work day?
> What must I learn?

Read, write, or teach at what level and for whom?

And so on....until you have your vision of the job, indicating what anyone may face in accomplishing its aims.

By using the reporter's information query method, applicants, even those without a particular job background, should be able to articulate undisclosed yet relevant factors to a position profile's objectives. Prospective employers can draw defensible criticism about job-seekers who fail or are unable to give thought to unstated aspects that connect to job objectives. "The applicant does not have a sincere interest or does not possess the knowledge and/or capability to meet job expectations." Why? Because an applicant makes inquiry to a prospective employer with the intent of personal gain in exchange for job services to be rendered later. Having ample time to study and consider appropriate associations with listed job objectives but not doing so says of the applicant, "Trust my intent while I discover our purpose." Why should your perspective employer (customer) trust your intent, given the fact you have failed to give acknowledgement to their written needs and purpose in the first place?

Acknowledgment is an admission that something expressed is recognized. By communicating personal thoughts about this new business opportunity, you show interest, motivation, discernment, and your possible usefulness in fulfilling job accountabilities. To a prospective employer and for a time after being hired, you are an uncertainty to them. You have your private motives for seeking particular employment, but to perform the job will require attention to those aspects that are job-related. Understanding the work's purpose, recognition of the work activities that must be performed, and performance achieve a result. Investing in your training may be a practical as well as a necessary consideration on the employer's behalf. The prospective employer is attempting to gauge your willingness, readiness, and ability to perform. Informal and formal learning is an integral part of human performance improvement. But in order to begin learning anything, one must first give attention to the subject—readiness to begin. An applicant's degree of readiness to do work can bear directly on employer's expense and ultimate hiring decision. Costs incurred for getting a new employee ready to perform at a certain level are variable. Obviously, applicants who can demonstrate a higher readiness to perform and learn would appear a lesser risk than others. Time costs money also.

8
Session Essentials

To this point, we have considered general employment and job interviewing assumptions and notions that commonly impact such practices. Characteristics of organizational work and individuals have also been explored, so that the applicant selection process could begin with a better perspective as to its true purpose and essential elements. Now the focus will shift to a more defined explanation of how the adoption of new conditions and methods can neutralize interviewer and applicant interview behaviors that are undesirable, raising the typically arbitrary activity of job interviewing to a higher systematic process standard for all.

Interview Scheduling Procedures

Proper scheduling of the interview session is an extremely important after the organization has properly prepared position profiles for the interviewer and applicant. Typically, the interviewer will contact the job candidate and schedule a time to meet. However, proceeding in that fashion would mean the laborious chore of preparing the applicant's Position Profile would have been for naught. Imagine the simple task of shopping for groceries to last a week or two. Persons customarily prepare a list of items in order to:

a) Know what items are needed.

b) Know what items are desired.

c) Get items in perspective as to what's more or less important.

d) Review and modify choices listed.

e) Have a reminder.

When grocery shopping for two or more, to leave the list at home and shop off the cuff can invite some criticism and frustration. "Where's the skim milk? Whole milk wasn't on the list!" Interviewers should send the applicant a position profile days prior to the interview session. Recall that conditions must support the interview's intent. Here, this supporting condition serves to direct both the interviewer and applicant away from feelings of what may be important and toward thoughts that are important—fulfilling future job objectives.

"Hello, Ms. Applicant, we've reviewed your resume and would like to schedule you for an interview. Are you still interested in the position?"

"Yes, I am."

"Do you have access to a fax machine or email? Because we would like to send you a position profile that list the typical objectives of the position. Our discussions during the interview will revolve around this profile, so it should be helpful to you."

"I don't have a fax machine or computer. Can you mail it to me, or may I pick it up?"

"We'll mail it to you. If you don't receive it within five days, please call me. Now, can we schedule your interview?"

Note: Previewing the position profile by the applicant in private prior to the actual interview is imperative. The question of how much preview time is ample is not so clear. The number of objectives, job complexity, prior history, and session time available should be weighed to determine whether this is days or minutes. Having more time than is needed is better than not enough time.

Later…Applicant receives prospective employer's form letter and the position profile.

Dear Applicant:

Enclosed is the position profile for your job interview. Please read it over and consider it very carefully. This profile and your application/resume will be the focus of your interview. Keep in mind that whether you have experience in any of the objectives as outlined or not, we want to know your impressions or thoughts about them.

For example, to operate a car in an empty parking lot is one thing. However, to drive it to a destination requires consideration of its condition, the driver's ability, others, traffic, signs, route, hazards, etc. We have given you our destination(s), and we would like to know your skill at driving on our behalf, as well as those personal and external factors that you think might affect your arrival. We are not looking for correct answers, just your sincere opinion.

If you have credentials or exhibits of your work, please feel free to bring them along.

Looking forward to discussing business with you.

Sincerely,

Recruiter

What reaction would applicants for any job have upon receipt of such a form letter and a position profile? First off, the applicant would know what's needed from them. Secondly, it places the burden of their employment intent squarely upon their shoulders. Sure, the employment situation could provide adequate pay, autonomy, benefits, and the like, but such considerations are based on the applicant's capability to render some clearly-defined services beforehand. "Can I do this, all of it, or some of it? Do I want to do this? Why or why not?" Thirdly, the applicant will understand that the employer wants him or her to share thoughts about achieving certain things on the employer's behalf. "Let me think about this for a while, because maybe I can and do want to do these things; they seem interesting, easy, important, creative, challenging, etc." Applicants who sincerely expect to earn their pay would welcome such up-front clarity. It gives them the opportunity to be truly job-focused during the interview and gives them a broader appreciation of their expected employment service. Then, too, the anticipated return on their personal investment can be weighed against realistic measures. "I don't think they (employer) will be paying minimum wage for such difficult work." Applicants who shop for opportunity without the intent of performing due diligence in the prospective job would also welcome such clarity. Their time and the interviewer's would not be wasted in discovering what it is they may not want to do, nor is their energy exerted towards a prospect for which they are unprepared or which they are unwilling to do and thereby cannot give critical thought to. By this method, applicants can pre-screen themselves.

Session's Intent

"Ms. Applicant, here's a copy of your resume and a copy of the position profile you received. Please feel free to reference either during our discussions, but you will not be allowed to reference or read from any other notes. Before proceeding further, the organization will pay a minimum of X dollars per hour. We offer the following benefits. I will be taking notes, as well as video-recording our discussion so that I can better reference your interview later. The recording will be erased at the conclusion of this selection process. Let me apologize before we get started: I may cut short some of your responses to certain questions in order to cover other questions in the time we have. Do you have any questions before we get started?"

- How do you rate your capability to accomplish the overall job objectives?
- For item thirteen, how has your knowledge or past experiences prepared you to handle it?
- Your resume indicates this. Does item two require closely similar activities? How?
- Item seventeen under "environmental and special conditions" states that out-of-town and overnight travel may be necessary. Would that be difficult for you?
- Item six requires some math skills, and there is a math aptitude test. How comfortable are you with figuring percentages and taking tests?
- Which, if any, items on the profile would pose the biggest learning challenge(s) for you?
- Eighty percent of activities require word processing skills. How many words do you type per minute?
- If you had to remove three items from this profile, which three would it be?"

And so on….

Here, the job interview's intent of conducting business is placed first and foremost in a serious manner. There is no need for introductory small talk or conversational patter to facilitate interpersonal familiarity. Communication is driven by and balanced on a mutually apparent and single subject for both interviewer and applicant. Question form can be tricky . For example, asking an applicant, "Tell me your business strengths?", would seem a justifiable inquiry. However, to applicant, the interviewer has pre-qualified the answer. Particular business strengths, useful business strengths, a certain number of business strengths, organizational business strengths, interviewer's business strengths, etc., may pose very different thoughts between interviewer and applicant.

By addressing the written job objectives contained in the position profile only, the interviewer eliminates presumptive qualifiers from their own speech. Moreover, the interviewer has minimized nonverbal signals to the applicant and has reduced the need for nonverbal synchrony from the applicant. The need for rapport is diminished, and information gathering as a function of time is increased. The applicant sees written, relevant job content in "black and white" and does not have to interpret the subjective viewpoint of an interviewer. David Olson (1986), remarking on the historical significance of the written word in communicating, wrote.

> Literacy changed language from an ephemeral means of communication to a permanent, visible object, the written word. Once the written word is seen as an object, the spoken word can be treated as an object. What are the properties of this object?.... Mental state concepts such as intend, interpret and infer come to be distinguished, as do speech act concepts such as assert, claim, state and declare.... These conceptual distinctions.... are extremely important in understanding a speaker's or agent's intentions relative to their utterances or actions.... (352-353)

This technique is similar to that used by therapists to encourage and better understand a patient's thinking without passing signals that may be construed by the patient as judgmental. Here again, the job of the interviewer is made much easier because dialogue is based on a mutual awareness of what's expected. Looking forward, the applicant is given a clearer view of the entire job, and the particular objectives can be considered individually. Listening to their perceptions and comments on different objectives is how interest and capability on the part of applicant for the overall job are most effectively discerned. The interviewer is considering three aspects of an applicant's response.

- Does the applicant express undisclosed factors that relate to job objectives?
- Does the applicant have the prerequisite knowledge, skills, and capability to perform?
- Does the applicant want to perform?

Applicant Responsiveness

By introducing questions based solely on a well-constructed position profile, ambiguity, intrusiveness, and nonsense queries common in traditionally-structured interviews can be eliminated. Previewing and referencing the profile by the applicant before and during the session accentuates the business of interviewing. Moreover, using this technique better compensates for varying degrees of attention deficits that are present in auditory senses as well as heightened streams of consciousness in interviewees.

An individual's perceptive characteristics are functions of sensory processes and streams of consciousness. As mentioned previously, to hear (sensory), to think (interpret and evaluate), and to verbally respond (send what message) are three complex and independent processes that are self-regulated and thereby function differently in individuals. By proceeding as described above, the meeting's intended message has been delivered to the applicant before an immediate response is needed. The applicant now has time to read, interpret, evaluate, imagine, and decide what verbal message response to the interviewer should be sent.

Paintings of an identical landscape by different artists may, for example, result in completely different renderings. Even if the same artist paints the same landscape again, the subsequent painting will differ from the initial work. New facts, different lighting, new expressions, new paint, and myriad other factors (the experiential experience) give rise to a different viewpoint. Remember, the object of the selection process is to identify the best candidate. By proper preparation and even-handedness, the interviewer will gain clearer insights into the skills, capabilities, and desires of each candidate being considered.

In the absence of standardization of questions, the failure to remember applicant responses and the careless ways in which replies are elicited and interpreted make an objective comparison of applicants more difficult. Using and conducting job interviews based on concepts and procedures as mentioned narrows the perceptual scope and sharpens clarity. The interviewer's second most critical task, after laying the position profile as foundation, is to erect a framework, one that will facilitate the interview process by coaching and prompting the applicant to expand on his or her responses to each objective.

Everything discussed thus far has led to the conclusion that a new way of job interviewing would be more beneficial to employers, interviewers, and applicants. Employers when considering hiring are obliged to follow a doctrine of organizational best interest. "Best interest" will now mean fulfilling written objectives. Determining to what degree an applicant will be most useful in achieving an employer's needs is all that remains in making such a connection.

Critical Thinking Conditions

As mentioned, thought processes of a problem-solving type do not attend to abstractions. In other words, when an individual focuses on a problem or a search for solution, they believe first that a solution is obtainable. Any exercise designed to infer an individual's problem-solving ability must have finality. With formal reasoning, this can often be an easy assessment through task design—for example, giving an individual a set of math problems to solve, then evaluating their performance for speed and accuracy in solutions. What about assessing productive thinking skills (informal) for general or real business challenges? In such cases, the interviewer should never present a hypothetical question or problem to an applicant and request a reasoned response. This mistake is most apparent in interviews where short, academic-type case problems are presented and applicants are asked to provide reasoned responses to the issue(s) contained within. Such exercises are useful tools for the classroom but are inappropriate in job interviews.

Without a position profile, the interviewer should always ask an applicant's impressions of a hypothetical question or problem. It is not correct answers, but the applicant's thought process as related to expected performance that is being evaluated. Whether an applicant is shopping for a different employer or in need of employment, they desire to make the best impression. Since an applicant will be new, asking them to respond with certitude to an imagined situation or circumstance without an envelope of reality is disingenuous. The interviewer will get two types of responses from interviewees if they are asked to solve a hypothetical problem—shallow or safe contrivance.

Incorrect Question: How would you increase sales?

Correct: What are your impressions of selling?

Answers: Hard, closing, attitude, training, initiative, boldness, planning, prospecting, persistence, baselines, winning, organizing, marketing, knowledge, tracking, etc.

Incorrect Question: What makes a good consultant?

Correct: Consulting has many aspects; what do you think about in terms of consulting?

Answers: Personalities, needs, knowledge, evaluating, coaching, facts, analyzing, designing, presenting, selling, training, etc.

Incorrect Question: Why should we hire you?/Tell me about yourself.

Correct: What impressions do you have of the job?

Answers: Intellectual, easy, busy, stressful, lots of issues, personnel problems, fast, slow, creative, routine, physical, political, long –hours, etc.

Job interviews must provide "free space" whereby effective expression is encouraged, particularly if an assessment of thinking skills is needed. Interviewers and applicants have misconstrued projecting a positive image to mean something other than effective capabilities to perform the job. The applicant may seem gift-wrapped or inept because they have been programmed into responding with boilerplate cliché. Competent interviewers must accommodate the business intent of the interview by leading the applicant away from pretext.

A distinguishing characteristic of expert problem-solvers, compared to novices, is that the former shows an increased capacity to generalize informational knowledge, retrieve relationships, and systematically reassemble variable factors in novel ways. Thus, an employer who wants an engineer to change duties and become a sales' consultant has to be certain that the engineer's attitude is inclined towards learning and adapting to the new work product with its associated conditions. Thinking, unlike physical actions, cannot be externally controlled. In the fiction movie, *Trading Places*, Wall Street brokers tried to explain the commodity trading business to an uneducated con man. The con man listened and replied, "I see, you guys run a bookie business. I can do that!"

Finally, in an attempt to gauge an applicant's productive thinking, it is extremely important that the interviewer establish an atmosphere conducive to dissent. Discourse without opportunity to disagree forms plans of action without weight. If the organization desires "those that can use their head," then attending to contradictions is a necessary exercise of problem-solvers that must be encouraged and addressed.

Interviewer: One of the challenges you will face as a production supervisor is training assembly line workers to reduce errors in workmanship.

Interviewee: Why is that a problem? Are your calibration settings inaccurate? How old are your machines? They may not be able to handle added unit rates. Training may not be the problem.

In the above exchange, the interviewee negatively dismissed the interviewer's concern and has already begun to explore other issues that may in his mind be affecting quality. The applicant is "thinking aloud".

Interviewer: I think we know what's needed! Can you train?

Interviewee: (Damn. They don't want me to think except about how and what they feel is important. I must be careful and not alienate myself.) Sure, sorry about that.

In one quick blunder, the interviewer's arrogance and impatience have shut down the applicant's verbal expressions of thought. The remainder of the interview will be reduced to attempts at contrived acquiescence on the part of the applicant, diminishing the prospects for a more objective appraisal of the applicant's productive thinking abilities. A failure to acknowledge and consider opposing viewpoints in business dialogue negates the thinking process, contributing to wasted time and misguided results. In contrast, a person's active participation in team sports or the military requires the suspension of personal uncertainty (thought) in favor of an orchestrated, often rehearsed, and immediate critical action. To the extent that productive thinking is relative to the fulfillment of work objectives, mental behaviors, along with physical behaviors, must be realized in association with them.

A Connective Interview Session

As the interviewer and applicant, using a position profile, move beyond the written objective, other, relevant questions and responses should arise. Interviewers must be cautious in characterizing applicant responses as declarations of certainty. Applicant responses represent clues as to how well he or she has considered and framed appropriate factors that may affect desirable work outcomes. Does the applicant have the ability and capability to perform as expected? How adaptable is his or her thinking, given what's expected? Do they demonstrate interest, originality, and sensibility to the written objectives, or are they attempting to establish rapport and concurrence with the interviewer? The position profile is "the thing," and it could serve the same purpose via telephone as it does in a face-to-face. However, a phone interview may prompt a scripted reading by an applicant, so this should not be done using a position profile. Remember, an applicant's ability to memorize is not what's being assessed.

In the following illustration, four candidates—A, B C, and D—are applying for the position of Newspaper District Manager as depicted in the position profile in figure 4-1. Assume that both A and D have no previous newspaper experience. Both B and C have had previous newspaper circulation experience. Each candidate will be asked the same initial questions in the same sequence, and their responses will be noted. This is a proper utilization of a position profile during an interview.

Asking an applicant at what level they rated their capability to perform the prospective job is the first information needed by the interviewer. It represents the applicant's degree of confidence in handling the job requirements, and the interviewer's final assessment of this factor should be comparable to the applicant's or something was amiss, meaning the applicant isn't ready, willing, or able to handle the job. After recording that rating, the interviewer can proceed to any of the objectives listed on the position profile. Remember, all applicants must be asked the same initial questions in the same order.

Interviewer's question to applicant: What are your thoughts and impressions of item three?

(3. Will use recruiting, screening and interviewing techniques for selecting contractors as needed.)

Responses:

Applicant A: Are they the same as newspaper carriers? What techniques do newspaper managers use? Do they run ads in the newspaper? I guess schools would be a good place to recruit teenagers. How young can a carrier be? What help will the newspaper give me? How many contractors will I need? Won't company training cover this subject? I'm not uncomfortable talking to people. I've run youth groups and organized fundraising drives for church. Also, I've done multilevel marketing recruitment.

Interviewer: Do you think you would prefer teenagers or adults as contractors?

Applicant A: I don't know. I think teenagers would stay longer. I mean, they have fewer options for making money.

Interviewer: What do you think a teenager might desire to earn at a minimum if they had to deliver early in the morning seven days a week?

Applicant A: I don't know. One of my older brothers had a route in high school. I think he made about $110 per week. He kept it almost two years until he graduated. Boy, he would complain about customers who didn't pay on time. I noticed in the job outline (position profile) that I collect from people, but I didn't see where I paid anyone. Why is that?

Etc., etc.

Applicant B: I try to establish a good relationship with my contractors and customers because I like to use them as referral sources. I have paid rewards to carriers and customers for their referrals that were contracted. I also use a phone list and door-to-door knocking to canvass my district for contractors. One of the hardest things for a carrier to do is wake up in the morning before sunrise and deliver consistently, day in and day out. The other difficulty is that a lot of carriers will give good service, but only a few put in a consistent effort selling. So, I try to screen for carriers to prevent those types of problems.

Interviewer: Was paying for referrals expensive, and how did it benefit you?

Applicant B: No, not really. It saved me a lot of time. Twenty dollars got me a prescreened carrier with a good recommendation. I made almost that much per hour. I think the secret to this work is time management.

Interviewer: How is time management important?

Applicant B: Everything is scheduled. Deliveries and collections have to be taken care of by a certain time. Contractors and customers have to go to work or school by a certain time. If you don't manage your time right, things get more complicated, causing other problems. I've known managers who work twelve hours a day with little to show but more problems. You have to work smart, not hard, or you'll burn out.

Interviewer: But unexpected things can happen?

Applicant B: Sure. But the only thing you know for sure is the schedule for the district. The unexpected will happen if it happens. You deal with it after meeting your schedule. Otherwise, you affect bigger things, like your whole district.

Etc., etc....

Applicant C: Business contacts and information like dealers, carriers, customers, phone lists, and the public have always been useful resources for finding carriers. As a new hire, would I be assigned a poor district—one with low profit routes, high crime, and high contractor turnover? If so, what type of incentives does the newspaper offer carriers? And how will my efforts be judged in comparison with more wealthy districts? Does the company reimburse me if I have to pay someone to temporarily throw a route, and for how long? Are all of your routes direct office pay or carrier collects? Does the company offer a bounty to existing carriers that find new carriers? Will they get up in time, do they have other commitments, how much money do they expect, is it a parent's wish or their child's wish, and will they have a substitute are some of the things I consider before signing a contractor.

Interviewer: How would a wealthier or poorer district effect your ability to perform?

Applicant C: It is not my ability, because I will do what's necessary to get the job done. But I am not naïve. Poorer districts require more maintenance and have more problems. The company can offer no support, a little, or a lot and I just want to know its position. I don't mind working hard, but if I am offered a district, I want to know the real deal.

Interviewer: I can say that the company offers special incentives to managers and contractors in districts defined as economically disadvantaged. Among such incentives are... If you are hired, the chance is great that you would be assigned such a district. Now, what problems do you think might be expected?

Applicant C: What I will be looking hard for is honest teenagers and adults. Crime, drugs, and fear tend to keep good contractors away. The ones you don't want will use the route as a quick hustle, steal the collection money, and stop delivering without notice. You have to keep a few aces available to continue delivery and maybe collections. Also, you get a lot of freebie customers who want the paper but do not intend to pay for it. That's why I asked whether carriers collect or the customers mail payments to the office. What is the company policy on customers who don't pay? How are my contractors affected by customers who don't pay?

Interviewer: I don't know. But I will find out and inform you if a further interview is warranted. Do you think you can handle a problem district, or want to?

Applicant C: I have. Once I understand the setup better and weigh my total compensation, I can tell you whether I want to.

Etc., etc....

Applicant D: Naturally, as a manager, I would want reliable workers. Are you a district manager or former one?

Interviewer: No.

Applicant D: Well, I guess it wouldn't be hard. I mean, kids are always looking to pick up extra money. Right?

Interviewer: I am not sure. Please go on.

Applicant D: As my resume indicates, I have excellent interpersonal skills and get along well with people.

Interviewer: I agree that is an excellent skill. How would you use that here?

Applicant D: I don't know—probably the newspaper could run a "help wanted" ad? It worked for me. The main thing is finding reliable kids that don't need a lot of money. My own kids cut grass in the neighborhood and do small errands to pick up spending money. I'm open to ideas.

Etc. Etc.

In these responses to the same initial question, different degrees of connectivity are evident. Notice how the interviewer's questions flowed from the applicant's responses and not the interviewer's opinion of what an applicant's responses should be. But what is most obvious is that the interviewer using a position profile and proper interview technique could not possibly write down the responses quickly or recall all of them in order to make a meaningful assessment later. Using a tape recorder or video camera to help capture expressions of thought is strongly recommended. This is indispensable when selecting candidates that will work under minimal or no direct supervision. Furthermore, interviewees can find it disconcerting watching a recruiter struggling to jot remarks and may instinctively shorten their own response out of politeness.

Connective's Purpose

As touched on in an earlier chapter, studies in the field of human performance technology consider three broad areas for assessing business activity or organizational performance. The environmental area is broadest in scope. It is indicative of upper management decision-making to include communication clarity, strategy, and commitment to accomplish objectives. Examples would be the allocation of management resources, such as knowledge, money, tools, materials, skills, and staffing to create efficiencies for performing activities and accomplishing goals. Also, autonomous external factors like market demographics that affect service and product acceptance are represented when evaluating the environment.

A second area given equal value in measuring performance is the performer (employee). Does the performer understand what is needed and how to accomplish it? Does he or she have the knowledge, enabling skills, and desire to perform? Thirdly, and of equal importance as the other two, is evaluating the job context. Whether the context under study surrounds sales, quality control, interviewing, processing speed, or other activities, it must be examined. What of the performance can be quantified or qualified? What can be reasonably expected given other factors, and what must be done to realize expectations, given the big picture? This triangular model used in performance assessing is a connective, and the stronger and more connectivity to the job a candidate demonstrates during an interview, the better the possibility of a successful employment situation on both sides.

In considering the responses of the four applicants above, it is noted:

Applicant A, with no prior experience in newspaper circulation, has given responses mostly related to procedural inquiry. Also, this applicant has related expressions of thought to aspects of the objective under consideration to undisclosed and concrete factors (advertising, schools, modeling of experienced managers, organizing people, communicating with strangers, payments, etc.).

Applicant B, an experienced district manager, responds by stating what he has done in the past in relating to the question. He also sheds some light on his philosophical attitude (what distinguishes a carrier, time management). Also, he implies willingness to display personal industry and initiative by using phone lists and knocking on customers' doors.

Applicant C an experienced district manager responds by stating what he has done in the past in relating to the question and asked questions of the interviewer. His questions show an understanding of the organization's influence on his job. What is management's philosophy and how does it implement it? He also displays discernment by relating undisclosed screening factors to not only prospective contractors' characteristics but their expectations (parent or child) as well. Further, some of the social and physical factors (job context) that interact directly with his performance are mentioned.

Applicant D with no prior experience in newspaper circulation responds on the basis emotional synchronicity and mimic. He has not considered the objective or cannot think of anything significant showing an interest in this objective. How does he know a 'reliable kid' when he meets one? Further, he has tried to steer the focus away from the business at hand attempting personal familiarity. Note how the interviewer keeps the focus on the objective by encouraging the applicant to give more information while being nonjudgmental. For this one objective, this applicant has shown more interest in the benefits of employment rather than providing a service to earn such benefits.

Depending on the number of objectives delineated in the position profile and time constraints, the interviewer may choose to limit focus on those objectives the organization finds most important. Also, if more than one interview session is scheduled for an applicant, questions can be divided among the sessions. Uniformity in the initial question presentation to all applicants must be maintained. There is no need to design extraneous questions with this approach. The applicant and profile carry the information, not the interviewer.

Applicant's Connective Ratings

Interviewers should avoid asking questions beginning with "why." Instead, use question forms such as "how," "interesting," "go on," "I see," "please continue," and other expressions that encourage the giving of information rather than the defense of information already provided. All initial questions that may be asked by the interviewer are relevant to specific activities comprising the job. The whole interview communication represents an intertwining of different nuances by an applicant. Each applicant's thinking, desire, ability, knowledge, versatility, motivation, and even attitude converge into uniquely useful displays and nuances.

Suppose in our example, the interviewer gave Applicant B a six on Monday and then interviewed Applicant C on Tuesday and wanted to give him a higher degree of connectivity with an objective than Applicant B. Such a situation would be expected to happen more frequently here than with a traditional interview technique. Because applicant responses are less constrained by convention, the interviewer has greater opportunity to hear originality. The objective's connectivity scale is a tool, but it is not a test. If the interviewer chooses to lower or increase the degree of connectivity of an applicant to a specific objective, so be it. The object is to select the best job candidate based on a more objective appraisal of applicant overall responses to each outcome and organizational determinants. Many interviewers use the three-pile approach to sort resumes. Pile one resumes are prized, pile two resumes are maybes, and pile three resumes are forgotten. The same sorting procedure can be utilized for completed position profile assessments.

Applicant A's connectivity

3. Will use recruiting, screening and interviewing techniques for selecting contractors as needed.

Low   0   1   2   **3**   4   5   6   High

Applicant B's connectivity

3. Will use recruiting, screening and interviewing techniques for selecting contractors as needed.

Low   0   1   2   3   4   **5**   **6**   High

Applicant C's connectivity

3. Will use recruiting, screening and interviewing techniques for selecting contractors as needed.

Low   0   1   2   3   4   5   **6**   High

Applicant D's connectivity

3. Will use recruiting, screening and interviewing techniques for selecting contractors as needed.

Low   **0**   1   2   3   4   5   6   High

Scoring Responses

General intelligence of a practical nature distinct, from creativity or formal reasoning, can also be evidenced through use of the position profile. The written objectives to be accomplished are clearly-defined outcomes that have a beginning and an end. To arrive at a conclusion, an applicant must first be aware of (selective attention) and then perform certain mental or physical behaviors. The organization knows the environment and states the objectives, whereas the applicant infers the environment and declares those objects and information that are relevant to him or her in achieving those goals. If those objects and information are not of a kind or degree necessary, then the interviewer may conclude the applicant is willing but not yet ready or able to function at the level of the organization's desired expectation(s). Thus, the organization must now answer, based on the evidence uncovered (applicant's interest, thinking, and other skills), who should be hired through balancing the organization's determinants.

Once the interviewer completes a connectivity sheet(s) for all applicants, various rating methods can be applied to arrive at the best candidate for the position. A simple summation of interviewee connectivity scores on objectives can be computed, and the candidate with the highest overall rating is ranked highest. Another approach would be to add different weights to different objectives. As mentioned, objectives can be rated for example from one to three. Those objectives of an easier or more simplistic nature are given a lower weight, whereas those requiring more thought complexity, effort, essential knowledge, motor skills, etc. are given higher value. By multiplying each interviewee's connectivity score on an objective by a corresponding objective's weight and then summing, a more meaningful validation can be gained. Thus, a candidate with an overall higher score is more representative of a value-added resource for the organization. Finally, based on the applicant's overall connectivity score, three employer's determinates are balanced to select the candidate(s) that will best fulfill the employer's needs.

9
Putting It All Together

Employer's Three Determinants

Applicants are hired in terms of what's most important from the organization's overall employment perspective:

- The work needed.
- The applicant's readiness to perform what's needed.
- The perceived benefit or cost to employer.

Will a decision to do or not do something, i.e. hiring a particular person instead of someone else, have a greater or lesser benefit/cost to the employer? This judgment is based on balancing the following three organizational determinants.

a) **The organization's short-term, critical or immediate need**. Given two applicants for a customer service position, one has a four-year college degree and the other possesses a high school diploma. The organization determines that data-inputting skill (speed and accuracy) is their most critical need and chooses the high school graduate for the open position. This choice was made because a much higher degree of competence in a specific behavior (motor skill or manual dexterity) was urgent.

b) **The organization's short-term return on investment**. Two candidates applied for the position of regional sales manager. One had extensive experience as a division warehouse and purchasing supervisor, and the other was a highly-successful commission salesperson. The organization chose the former, although he had never sold products or services. Although the open position title referenced sales, the critical skill sets desired were personnel supervision, fact finding, and customer support systems. The organization already had sales personnel and concluded that someone with demonstrated accomplishments in those other areas would give a quicker return on investment. In the parlance of instructional developers, one of the applicants displayed more enabling skills, so the learning curve in manipulating external factors to increase overall performance should be smaller. Another approach under this determinant would be to hire based primarily on labor cost or hire at lowest cost.

c) Hiring "those that can use their head" (Potentials/Leaders)

Type A applicant has established skills and similar environmental experience in dealing with most or all job objectives as outlined in a position profile—they are willing, ready, and able to perform immediately. This type of candidate can discuss, explain, or demonstrate required procedural and conceptual competency with a high degree of credibility.

Type B candidate has established skills for accomplishing some or most job objectives as outlined in a position profile, but lacks specific environmental or job context experience—they will need time to learn environmental and conditional factors. This type of applicant can discuss, comprehend, or demonstrate principles inherent to fulfilling job needs. They are willing and able, but will need time to be ready.

Type C applicants pose no particular difficulty in hiring, but may be the hardest to manage. Robert Sternburg (1988) distinguished three aspects of intelligence, of which two have particular import for work environments. Experiential intelligence has to do with how well an individual can transfer skills to new situations. Persons lacking in experiential intelligence perform well only under a narrow set of circumstances, whereas others demonstrate ability to quickly comprehend and learn new tasks. For example, a worker who has done routine assembly work is promoted to supervisor. Now that same worker must do emotional work—that is, the supervising of others. How well the worker copes and quickly effectuates his new task is an indication of his experiential intelligence. The other intelligence Sternburg theorized is termed contextual intelligence. Tacit knowledge is characterized by informal reasoning strategies for success that are not explicitly taught but are inferred from observations, and without contextual intelligence, you cannot acquire it (Sternberg et al. 1995). In studies of salespeople and business managers, tacit knowledge was shown to be a good predictor of job effectiveness (Sternberg, Wagner, and Okagaki, 1993). Critical thinking is a solitary pursuit, and thus will be less dependent on external management justification or prompting. Those who practice higher levels of critical thinking can discern message validity and gauge problems more easily than those who don't. Consequently, those who supervise critical thinkers often have problems leading them. Team play, or concurrence, is a group process or procedure adopted for efficiency in order to derive a result. A critical thinker may have the smarts to generate novel ideas and strategies but lack the people smarts and/or patience to maximize a work group's operations (efficiency) or accept poorly-constructed thought in a superior. This type of applicant offers divergent thinking and innovation and tends to pose probing questions directed at purposed outcomes and procedures. They must believe that they possess the basic skills to do a job and have an interest in doing so. Applicant responses that demonstrate a breadth and depth of relevant factors to an objective should be in evidence here.

Interviewer: I'm sorry, but I don't think you can handle this job.

Applicant: Why not?

Interviewer: You lack experience in this type of work environment.

Applicant: So, Henry Ford introduced the automotive assembly line, Thomas Edison invented the light bulb... I could go on. The point being, my lack of experience has little to do with me accomplishing the activities discussed. It's not brain surgery.

Interviewer: Yeah, but you don't know calculus.

Applicant: You're right. Thank you for the interview.

In the above exchange, the interviewer created "free space" by challenging the interviewee within the job content. The interviewer raised a concrete job objection, the lack of a defined and essential skill. "Those that use their heads" enjoy using their heads. Potential and leadership are a willingness, readiness, and ability to achieve in spite of circumstances. Klemp and McClelland (1986), in a written perspective based on comprehensive research studies, reported the following: Among eight identified competencies which differentiated outstanding senior managers from mediocre ones, self-confidence was shown to be the most prevalent among all high performers. These researchers further noted that crises and other problems, rather than creating anxiety or stress in the outstanding managers, caused them to feel excited and challenged. It is important to note that, based on determinants, a trainee may be considered a better choice than an experienced applicant in terms of potential and leadership.

Connective's Improvements

The connective interview technique is structured and job-centered, and requires considerations based on relevant job-related aspects only. It is developed and designed from a systems theory model wherein the work environment, performer, and job context are objectively interconnected not only with the position under consideration but, as importantly, with the interview session itself. As a job-interviewing technique, some of its unique highlights are:

- It is tailored to advance relevant interview objectives and not speculations.
- It is easy to construct, more practical, and more adaptable.
- It suppresses the entry of communicative biases.
- Applicant is given interview's intent and must engage employer's needs before personal ones.
- Critical thinking is better evidenced because more time is available for consideration.
- Both parties (interviewer and applicant) have a mutual frame of reference.

Figure 9-1 is a chart comparing well-known interview methods with the new connective interview method through ten sequential steps commonly followed in all types of job interviews. Read the chart by beginning with step one in the middle column. Then compare the contrasting columns on both sides of the middle column for each sequential step. This shows the connective interview's approach and methodology to be superior to other employment type interviews.

Figure 9-1

Comparison of Image-Type versus Connective Interview Process

Image-Type Interviews Aspects	Sequenced Steps of Job Interview Process	New Connective Interview Aspects
Structured Personality/behavioral typing Critical incident approach Situational approach consisting of generalities, vagueness, abstractions	**STEP 1** Employer needs employee? or Employer needs job filled?	Structured Employer crafts written position profile (PP) based only on specific, clear, manifest expectations
Employer screens resumes based on assumptions	**STEP 2** Applicant submits resume/application because of interest in employment considerations and/or performing job?	Employer screens resumes against job objectives
Phone/mail notification	**STEP 3** Interviewer schedules applicant interview	Phone/mail notification with written interview guidelines and PP
Weaknesses: Subjective biases, irrelevancies, pre-qualified answers, disconnected from real job and applicant	**STEP 4** Employer creates interview questions: A complex and presumptive activity	Not applicable
Uncertainty of presentation and appraisal aspects	**STEP 5** Applicant prepares for interview	Critical thinking time Applicant reviews and considers PP factors
Strangers seeking commonalties and concurrence through non-verbal synchronicity and discourse Q & A Interviewer-centered	**STEP 6** The interview session: Of short, critical duration for conducting mutual business only	Strangers discussing evident business considerations through mutually-anticipated Q & A Tape or video recorder Job-centered

Figure 9-1 Continued

Image-Type Interviews Aspects	Sequenced Steps of Interview Process	New Connective Interview Aspects
Auditory reception only Assumed synchronicity of focus Assumed message clarity Interviewer-centered	**STEP 7** Interviewer chooses initial questions	Auditory and visual Reception Anticipated focus Relevancies only Mutually-observed message Job-centered
Seeks rapport and acceptance Assumes short response interval Anticipates a judgment Interviewer-centered	**STEP 8** Applicant's response	Expresses thoughts Response interval open-ended Interviewer facilitated Job- and Applicant-centered
Auditory selectivity narrow Subjective bias Short-term memory capacity Speed and accuracy of writing Interviewer focus distracted	**STEP 9** Interviewer notes applicant's responses	Auditory selectivity broader Message content objectivity Quantity and quality relevancy appraisal connectivity scale
Gut Feelings Arbitrary Lower Predictability Analysis	**STEP 10** Interviewer's Evaluation	Quantified & Qualified Measures Uniform Methodology Actual review ability Higher Predictability Analysis

Prepared, delivered, and assessed as outlined, the connective interview creates a different hierarchy, as shown below. That can markedly improve job interviewing by minimizing natural tendencies to infer and convey unwarranted aspects to a critical business selection process. Meaningful discovery and discussion for both interviewer and applicant are thereby facilitated.

Traditional's Incorrect Hierarchy	Connective's Corrected Hierarchy
• Interview presentation • Perceived affinity • Abilities and capabilities: Motor and other enabling skills Experience Knowledge Adaptability Thinking • No measures • Applicant interest and intent	• Numerical measures Quality Quantity • Evaluation methodology • Computer-adaptable • Employer's priorities: Job Objectives Determinants • Applicant interest and intent • Abilities and capabilities Thinking Motor and other enabling skills Knowledge Experience Adaptability • Interview presentation

Compared to image or traditional interviewing methods. The new connective interview process is:

- Convenient to administer
- More adaptable
- More effective
- Standardized
- Job and business-centered
- More efficient
- Computer-friendly
- Fairer

Case Study

A department in a large organization sought to hire an additional intermediate manager (IM). The hiring department's administrator ordered two intermediate and two senior managers (SM) from his department to form an interviewing committee to interview, evaluate, and recommend the top applicants for a final interview with him. The human resources department (HR) posted and made the open position available only to the organization's approximately 15,000 employees. HR screened all resumes and applications and only forwarded ten of the most qualified applicants as being eligible to be interviewed. The hiring department's committee created a position profile with eight job objectives, each having a four-category applicant response scale (excellent, competent, limited, unqualified) based on existing HR policy. The ten applicants, four from within the hiring department and six from other departments within the organization, were scheduled alphabetically for interviewing over a four-day period.

Each applicant was given written instructions, the position profile, and ten minutes in private before interviewing began. The written instruction given was, "The following job objectives will be the basis of your interview. We would to like to hear *your* thoughts, opinions, and/or examples of how you and/or undisclosed factors may affect your achievement of them. We are not interested in merely 'correct' answers." After ten minutes, the interviewers entered the room and introduced themselves. It was explained that this would be a two-step interview process and that each interviewer would randomly be asking questions and taking notes based on the applicant's comments on each job objective on the list. Then later, each interviewer would individually rank each applicant. The rankings would then be averaged together to provide a single committee ranking and given to the department's administrator, and at his discretion, applicants would be chosen for a final interview.

Interviewers were told that the strategy was to get as much information as possible and cautioned not use "why" or otherwise put an applicant on the defensive. After all applicants had been interviewed, each manager would submit a written ranking of all ten applicants. Managers were further instructed to use an applicant's responses, resume, application, or combinations thereof as a means of determining an applicant's rank. One number from one to ten could only be used to rank each applicant, no ties allowed, with one being the best qualified. Each manager's rankings were then inputted on a spreadsheet to arrive at an average committee ranking of each applicant. The names across the top row are manager interviewers, and (S) next to a name means senior manager. The left column, shows the applicants' names, and (E) means an employee from outside the hiring department. Figure 9-2 is the committee's ranking sheet that was given to the administrator for consideration.

Figure 9-2

	Rick(S)	Bill(S)	Tom	Joe	Final
Dave	2	2	3	1	2.0
Helen	1	1	2	5	2.3
John(E)	4	4	1	3	3.0
Gill	7	6	4	2	4.8
Sally(E)	5	5	5	4	4.8
Betty(E)	3	3	6	8	5.0
Gail	8	7	7	6	7.0
Jack(E)	6	8	8	7	7.3
Kevin(E)	9	9	10	9	9.3
Ted(E)	10	10	9	10	9.8

Background on participants and interview observations:

- Applicants Gill and Gail worked under intermediate supervisor Joe.

- Applicant Dave worked under senior Rick.

- Applicant Helen (the most recent department hire) worked under intermediate Tom.

- Three of the externals and two of the internal applicants were in the process of or had written notes on their profiles when the interviewers entered to begin the session.

- Each interview lasted thirty to fifty-five minutes, based on the same eight written job objective statements provided each applicant. Most applicants expressed similar and commonly held viewpoints. Only four applicants provided unique and more expansive responses.

- Joe took no notes and scored each objective for an applicant immediately after he or she finished a response.

- The other three managers wrote notes and scored applicants sometime later.

- Note taking was difficult; because all applicants said a lot and some spoke faster than others.

- All applicants seemed to become more relaxed after responding to the first objective, as evidenced by body language and speech.

- After all the objectives had been responded to, the applicants were asked if they had any comments or questions.

- Only one applicant said anything that was profoundly stupid. Ted, who had done okay in his responses to the objectives, afterwards made the following closing comment and inquiry: "One of my coworkers worked in this department some time ago. She said you have high turnover. Is that true? Because I don't want to walk into any problems." Bill answered, "We'll try hard not to cause you any problems."

- There was unanimous agreement among the interviewers that Kevin and Ted seemed the least qualified for the position of intermediate manager.

After the department's leader had a chance to review the committee's rankings, he called a meeting with his four managers to discuss it. His main concerns focused on the intermediate managers' ranking of applicants Betty, Gill and Helen.

The seniors described Betty's responses as model, confident and insightful. The intermediates described Betty as arrogant and someone whose past work experience wasn't close enough to the type of work done in this department. When the head asked the intermediates what they thought Betty lacked, they responded that they just didn't believe she'd work out well. The boss then switched his attention to Joe's rankings of Helen and Gill.

"I'm puzzled: why is your ranking of Helen and Gill so different than the other managers'?"

"That's just my opinion, sir."

"Explain it."

"Helen has only been here a short time, and I don't think it would be fair to our employees with more seniority…."

"Fair! Did she seem better qualified?

"Sir…."

"What about Gill? I know he's messed up things a few times in the past. But he works under you, doesn't he?"

"Well, everybody makes mistakes…."

"This meeting is over. Joe, I don't know where you're at, but I do know I don't like what I've heard from you, especially since your title is manager."

Tying Loose Ends

Is the new, Connective interview method good for employer/applicant business? The ability to preview job objectives undoubtedly gives all job candidates an identical opportunity. as would the traditional interview practice of not providing applicants such an opportunity. Those who would be expected to do well communicatively in the connective's absence should continue to do so. Those less talented at projecting the right image and interpersonal communication should fare better. Therefore, the connective would enable a more equitable opportunity for all applicants to do business.

All applicants? A critical premise that has underlined the need and importance for changing practices is that the interviewer and applicant are strangers. As in the case study, an employer may simultaneously extend a job opportunity to both external applicants and internal employees. With this as an interview situation, a portion of the applicant pool would naturally be tainted with a higher degree of management/employee biases. Thereby creating an advantage or disadvantage for some due to a common work history. Promotional (internals) and new hires (externals) must not be evaluated against one another. In large organizations with distinct departments, this prohibition would mean that employees within the hiring department should be not evaluated against employees from other departments. Employers must make a decision to either promote from within or to hire externally. A common difficulty is that a current employee seeking promotion has been predisposed to management's thought conformity and compliance. Yet the same management that wants new critical thinking or fresh perspectives feels compelled to look outside its own personnel, carelessly forgetting its own behavioral role in shaping an employee's past job performance. Further, this employee may feel uneasy in expressing business candor because he or she fears the possibility of disfavor or retribution from management. The irony is that the stellar but unknown new hire has a fifty-percent chance of becoming an average employee because of poor management. Christopher Columbus abandoned common sense and found land, not the abyss. Common sense may be commonly understood, but also may not be true or sensible. Balancing the three employer determinants is also a helpful exercise before deciding between promoting current employees and hiring new ones.

From the employer's perspective, the beginning question is also one of desired applicant capabilities. What type and degree of applicant work capability is important from the employer's job viewpoint? As mentioned, there are only two distinct types of employment work: emotional and non-emotional. An argument against the connective could be stated as follows: Traditional interview methods provide the employer a better opportunity to see how an applicant may react to the unexpected. They provide a chance to observe an applicant's responses when faced with a required but dubious question presentation. Can the applicant control her thinking, words, voice, and mannerisms to deliver messages so that they are received in an acceptable way? Such acting ability could allow a prospective employer to better achieve a particular business agenda.

What are the job requirements? Is an interviewing mix more in keeping with the employer's best business interest? It has been acknowledged that certain jobs like selling, direct customer servicing, and counseling have strong emotional work components. Policymaking, planning, processing, innovation, and so forth require less emotional play. If emotional work were the chief or only consideration for job accomplishment, then the recommendation would be for the interviewer to continue with traditional interview methods for those cases, keeping in mind the limitations that one's training and experience may place on devising and judging such an effort effectively and correctly. As shown, the connective can be introduced in full, as a mix, and as a series of step interviews from initial screening to a final, depending on the employer's interest. Applicant resumes/applications or employee performance appraisals can also be used in conjunction with the position profile.

Quality of leadership by interviewers and management is not evidenced by way of leadership title. Skills, knowledge, intelligence, and motivation are individual potentials that affect results. Education and experience are often overstated prerequisites for some jobs, especially those that don't require procedural competency. The ability to think critically, by its nature, is a solo pursuit. Those who lead others best are more keenly aware of this fact and adjust their own behavior to accommodate successful business opportunities.

As the case study showed, to leave the interview, any interview, unaccountable can result in poor decision-making. If there is one lesson to be gained here, it is that, despite the application of best practices, it is also prudent for employers not to leave the interview process neglected. Did Tom and Joe feel jealous or threatened by Helen? Why didn't Joe take notes on the applicants? Organizations must look to see what's going on behind closed doors from time to time, as well as examine the reasoning behind interviewers' choices. Some do not, and they may be paying for this omission big time.

Summary Thoughts

As I struggled, my body sweating despite the frigid temperature, to shovel ten inches of snow from my driveway one early morning, my neighbor's young child yelled, "Hey mister, you working or playing?"

"Work is work if you would rather be doing something else," remarked Mort Crim, a Detroit media personality. A particularly profound statement, I thought, succinctly differentiating between one's interest in a pursuit and the obligation of a pursuit. Whether the U.S. president or a homeless and destitute soul, one must fulfill needs occasioned not by choice. The employer-employee relationship is an arrangement of joint necessity. It is a quid pro quo proposition. Individuals on both sides may discover some aspects to be special within this arrangement, but that is not the reason for entering the agreement. Employment in the United States is unique and has evolved for better or worse because of individualism and not collectivism. This book has been prefaced on those realities.

Three significant business changes occurring over the past thirty years have altered the common perception of the U.S. employment landscape. First, new technologies have not only changed how we work, but raised business information from a narrow focus to a more general range of possibilities. The business phrase "multi-tasking" aptly expresses that change. Secondly, major U.S. industries have steadily moved away from a position of economic patriotism to one of expanding wealth opportunities via globalization. This goes way beyond economic pragmatism—goods and services to new market areas. Big businesses' drive for increased profit margins through lower labor costs, financial investing, inter-company leveraging, bartering for more favorable regulatory climates, and so forth have contributed to an epidemic of consciousness throughout the U.S.—expediency. The past illusion of a long-term bond between those in a company has been replaced by the reality of economic uncertainty, spurring greater impatience and a closer reliance on self-preservation. For far too many employees, their cynicism, skepticism, and anxiety seem a nearer occupation than their vocation. Expediency as the unexpected consequence of the other two has made traditional interviewing practices obsolete.

Complacency is no longer viewed as a satisfactory condition in or out of employment. Downsizing, right-sizing, restructuring, re-engineering, and privatizing were seldom considered or communicated prior to the1970s. Since a willingness to enter organizational employment holds no special uniqueness, in that most people choose such arrangements, work value can be the only distinguishing characteristic appraised by employers and demonstrated by employees. The possibility of achieving a standard in work value within an organization is degraded if such value has not been carefully communicated, qualified, and quantified. Unlike some computer or device, the functionality of an individual is not obvious. Inanimate things can be aligned to a specific task(s) because their properties are known to fit the task. On the other hand, strangers seeking employment may be well-suited for the task of being interviewed while being less effective than others in performing future employment tasks. Interviewer and applicant may each have unique interest, values, attitudes, and abilities, but only that table before them is a shared reality. To move beyond this situation without pretensions requires a communicative opportunity that replaces appearances of interviewer superiority with one favoring neutral ground.

Transparency of mutual intents is based upon a common apparent factor. For employers and applicants alike, this is an applicant's ability to accomplish a prospective employer's work. Adults should be clearly informed as to what is to be accomplished on behalf of an employer; the interview is not an exception. Most applicants and employees want to measure up. Therefore, selection processes and evaluations must have transparent merit.

"I can do the job" or "I do my job" are declarations of applicant or employee opinion. Evidence to the contrary must be based on the most objective and relevant appraisal available. Spoken words can be difficult or easy, offering many shades of reasoning and meaning. Employment is based on finite definitions of business intent and consists of action(s) arriving at an outcome(s). What an employer wants from a worker is their best work. What a worker wants from their employer is the best consideration(s) for providing it. There must be evidence in support of both desires. As an employee, one cannot be expected to do what is beyond one's ability, but an employee can be asked to do what they do not desire. If what is demanded is not illegal, immoral, unethical, or unsafe, on what grounds might an employee object? Maybe on the basis of convenience—infringing upon an employee's personal time, for example. Such a demand by an employer may be warranted; so also would be a worker's feeling of being imposed upon by such an edict. Clearly, the employee has not only the right of dissent, but more importantly, such a feeling should not come as a surprise or an affront to the employer, given the implied employment agreement. Employers acquire work service and not individuals. Employees are resources and not assets. For both, if only choices were free!

The stable, long-term workforce and employer relationship of past U.S. generations is becoming rare. As more employers eliminate employment needs and reduce commitments to workers, the labor market continues to grow from castaways and first-timers. Career paths with a single organization are becoming more tenuous also. As transient workers grow in numbers, employers will become less reliant on traditional, long-term workforce projection plans. Instead, employers will rely on fast-track recruitment action plans. Wise individuals will prepare themselves accordingly by indicating a serious and realistic presentation of their critical abilities and readiness to perform or opt to develop self–employment opportunities. Manpower Incorporated, a staffing firm, surpassed General Motors as the largest private organization with a workforce in the U.S. some years ago. Increasingly, this trend is becoming a business norm, and individuals will exit organizational employment jobs with increasing frequency.

What many astute U.S. business leaders have begun to realize is this revolving-door employment phenomenon has adverse implications for an organization's functional integrity. Employers must continually reinvest in training and development programs to maintain and improve work standards. Newly-trained workers are more likely than in the past to take recently-acquired skills to a different employer. Since loyalty has no context beyond an uncertain term. Workers too will remain forever vigilant to market advantage or, in business parlance, increased profitability. As the pool of transient workers grows, the reservoir from which core employees have been traditionally promoted shrinks. Sameness in business values and philosophy amongst core members will become less significant and more disparate. Effective decision-makers will have to look beyond their noses to find the abilities, reasoning, and creativity needed to sustain organizational improvement and growth. Just as organizations are driven by market potentials, they in turn must seek workers from the available labor market, further complicating matters. Unprepared management will remain preoccupied with personal issues and social maintenance in an attempt to salvage a body politic, entrapping them in a continuing melodrama of personal illusions instead of business pragmatism and thus drawing more and more energy away from their prime purpose of existence—external transactional gains.

The crux of problem is not how to retain good employees. Sound reasoning, incentives, and negotiations have proven effective and will continue to be effective retention strategies that may accomplish that on a case-by-case basis. The problem for organizations is how to minimize internal energy loss in selecting new employees while maximizing the potential of energy gains by better predicting successful work outcomes from applicants. Individual predictability is no different than business predictability; circumstances can result in unexpected changes. Nevertheless, careful planning and implementation to arrive at clearer expectations in hiring make much better sense than no plan at all. Arriving at friendship or, to a lesser degree, social affinity is something that cannot be planned unless one's intention is to date.

As advents in technologies have helped to change the employer/employee work relationship, they can also be utilized to more objectively assess and measure applicants for employment opportunities. Computers, tape recorders, video cameras, transcribers, and software are readily available tools that can help make the interview process more deliberate and manageable. Interviewers who will drive this updated process must first apply their energies to designing a blueprint of relevant and concrete work objectives to arrive at representative and functional position profiles. Finally, they must conduct a connective interview session to diminish the entry of biases and irrelevancies from both sides of the table. They must understand that, although personality traits of an individual may be positive or negative as well as consistent over time, attempts to predict the real disposition of a potential hire on hasty and poorly-substantiated judgments is of itself a negative behavior needing modification.

Management sets the work specifications and performance standards. Consequently, evaluating and clarifying what is needed to achieve desired outcomes must approximate the best in possibilities from that perspective. However, expectations by employers, which go beyond work activities to arrive at some personal or philosophical extravagances for applicants or their employees, are foolish. A new hire is an excellent employee, period. They are not average or poor. They were hired because expectations of capabilities to perform at a defined level were met. It's the work and work behavior of the employee, not the individual, that will be addressed. Prying into, speculating about, or seeking to modify an applicant's or an employee's private motives is as egregious as condoning, ignoring, and accepting poor work behavior and results would be. The priority should be on clarifying the facts in the business matter and then addressing performance by ascertaining the best in possibilities stemming from those facts.

U.S. employment represents a legal business arrangement of interactive work performances for individual personal gain having manifest, variable, and finite intents. Motives in employment which attempt to introduce and appraise such notions as personality, organizational commitment, family, thought conformity, intelligence, cohesiveness, and attitudes are personal/social biases rather than facts. More importantly, the brief interplay during an interview session offers little credibility to such assessments. Interview presentation emphasis, personality/behavioral typing, interpersonal communication, irrelevancies, personal affinity/concurrence, and perceptual ambiguities during the job interview can lead to unqualified business judgments.

Sensible Job Interviewing: Understanding the Employer's Role and Responsibilities has sought to wrestle the applicant and employer business relationship away from aspects of personality and common social interaction that more correctly reside outside a uniquely business arrangement. It has attempted to illuminate a space where strangers meet and make visible those obstacles that hinder mutually realistic viewpoints.

Employers have found in these pages:

- How to minimize interviewing arrogance and nonsense.
- A proactive and realistic written assessment of what is to be accomplished in an interview.
- How to develop job objectives.
- A means of assessing how personnel are being utilized.
- A means of assessing skill development needs.
- A standard evaluation system for all job interviewing.
- A broader rationale for making applicant choices.
- Greater opportunity to quantify information collection and selection criteria.
- Expanded opportunities to review actual interview process effectiveness and improve upon it.

Interviewers have found in these pages:

- How and why applicants may display certain behavior.

- How to prepare for an interview.
- How to properly conduct a session.
- How to increase pertinent applicant information per time.
- How to narrow personal and broaden business focus.
- How an applicant's employment versus work intent is better evidenced.
- How evaluations can be quantified and qualified based on measures.

Applicants have found in these pages:

- What employment means.
- What should be expected during an interview.
- How to best prepare for various interviewing approaches.

This book does not pretend that working relationships, once begun, will offer ample provisions and value throughout employment's term to all those concerned. But at the very least, there should be less confusion in the beginning as to how employer and employee are connected and what will be needed to sustain each other's company in the future.

Afterthought

This real-world alternative to traditional job interviewing practices has addressed considerations that are fundamental to relations between individuals engaged in organizational employment. Like a pick-up game, the preceding was merely a snapshot of one activity related to an official sport's grand design, rules, and regulations. Those major league games performed in global arenas at the highest levels—national economies. For me, this bigger picture, an economy at large, is key to improving employment and business opportunities generally. After reading this cursory postscript, some readers may also feel compelled to give a little thought as to what an economy should mean ideally. Others may be more inclined to delve deeper into matters of how an economy can best function and help make that happen. Discovering that its most significant characteristic is based on applied theory and is therefore always a trial and error proposition—experiment. With any experiment, assumptions underlying its theory are tested on the basis of environmental conditions present or unscientific beliefs chosen. Though only a select few can alter a society's economic workings, we are all subject to its trials, regardless of results and personal interest.

Much of what we know and think can be done is constrained by our mental sets or familiar thoughts. We coast along in our life's journey and at times have heard that familiar admonishment, "There's no need to reinvent the wheel." Henry Ford introduced revolutionary manufacturing processes around the early twentieth century. Nations centuries earlier began global exploration and established far-flung settlements. There have been thousands of similar life-changing events throughout history. Each, in passing, has caught and held societies to its common theme. New processes, activities, things, and concepts were instituted not because some persons sought change. Instead, changes occurred to them because something could be changed. Thank God, our cars are no longer driven about on wooden spokes.

Is the United States, or any nation, bound to its current economic system simply because, like the traditional job interview, that's how it is? Will there be enough employment and enterprising opportunities for this nation's citizenry? What should become of those unable to earn enough income to support themselves or families? As argued, those concerns are not within the purview of employers to resolve. That onus is upon governmental leadership, who would prefer, it seems, to acknowledge that only one problem exists by continually lamenting, "We need more job creation." What's the plan for addressing our citizens' quality of life concerns if more well-paying jobs are not created? In fact, job creation, upon closer examination, is not where the focus should be from a governmental viewpoint. It is more prudent to assume that not enough well-paying jobs will ever be created within our nation to adequately support a sizable majority. By stating the situation in this fashion, a worst-case scenario becomes the problem to address and manage.

Employment is not a need, but rather a means of fulfilling employer and individual needs. Historically, each succeeding generation has become more dependent on commercialization in order to fulfill needs and desires, whether simple or extravagant. Government, any government's, merit is defined by how well it administers justice and protection to all those it governs. Businesses and individuals are subject to policies, practices, and regulations imposed. Each may have different ideas as to what's personally desirable or just. We do not develop equally nor have identical motivations. One's degree of wealth or poverty is essentially the interplay of fate, circumstances, and motivations. What, then, from a governmental viewpoint, is economic justice, and how should it be administered? To be born into wealth or poverty requires no effort—it is fate. To live or die in wealth or poverty is causality—fate and circumstances. Wealth and poverty are relative terms, to be certain, and are of little help in defining what economic justice is or should be. But causality is reliant upon action or inaction to effect an outcome. So economic justice is best defined as an economic opportunity. Trade in goods and services have always been a utilitarian proposition. Gradually, trade has become a more speculative exchange buoyed by financial probabilities, rather than sales and buys anchored in reality. Injustice and malfeasance arise when incorrect principles limit and adversely alter trade opportunities in real time and value. The best economic system would maximize circumstances by which a motivated individual could take advantage of economic choices for fulfilling their quality-of-life concerns as quickly as possible based on real supply and demand cost.

Arguments about the redistribution of wealth assume that acquiring money capital, rather than personal access to societal opportunities, is or should be a universally-held ambition. Under this concept, individual pursuits of food, healthcare, knowledge, sanitation, education, leisure, family, and those other aspects of living are predicated on having money. Worldwide, most money is a discretionary unit of measure without intrinsic value. It is termed "fiat money" and relies on faith to function and support commerce exchange. Is a widget worth one dollar, or is one dollar worth a widget? Like the reader, I honestly don't know. Yet, I may be persuaded to sell each of my widgets for one dollar apiece. Not interested in buying a widget from me for one dollar? How about my vehicle? Most readers would probably jump on such an offer. But what if my selling price were changed to a much larger dollar amount? At some amount, prospective buyers would decrease. First, the profit takers would forsake interest—those seeking to resell my car. Then the bargain seekers would diminish—those that budget dollars. Finally, the only prospective buyers remaining would be those who really want my car and believe my price makes personal economic sense. This remaining group makes what economists call "the real economy." This type of market exchange is value- but not finance-driven.

Like in the board game Monopoly, where its property listings, houses, and hotels are the operative values, the real economy causes the trade upon which money is gained and lost. At the start of the game, all players have a somewhat equal chance, those first to toss the dice having a better chance. As the game progresses, those without the right values and luck lose money at a faster rate. If the same players simultaneously play two boards, the overall playing time is increased and the money fluctuations do not occur as rapidly.

In our real world, the real market economy of exchanging valued goods and services can be boundless. But speculative characteristics and premiums of financial/money industries have made comparative values in real commerce deformed while also effectively decreasing a more expansive and natural flow of exchange among a larger group of individuals. The real problem is not in that the "haves" possess too much and the "have nots" possess too little. It is their extreme social and economic estrangement in the community marketplace, or the real economy. Unwittingly, each one's condition and action being manipulated by money increases and decreases without any goods or services being exchanged in the real economy.

Who would begrudge a Henry Ford, Martha Stewart, Bill Gates, or Oprah Winfrey their wealth, seeing that tangible products and services by such persons derived understandably profitable exchanges from the real economy? They made wealth happen for themselves by producing and selling something. Some without such means may be resentful or jealous that those opportunities to experience the conditions of such wealth seem personally unreachable. I believe that most of us without such massive wealth accept such material distinctions while realizing we may need something more to have that certain level of comfort and security in our own respective lives. It could be a bigger house, more education, better health access, leisure time, fewer expenses, or combinations of whatever. Seemingly, then, fiat money and that other currency, "credit paper," are really outside our real goals or interest.

America's founding fathers had a much easier environmental situation to deal with economically than their present-day counterparts have. Land, food, and provisions for shelter or the basics for fulfilling human needs were in abundance and accessible to all. There was no need for an economic system per se. Also, the architects of our early government were special individuals due to one personally unique circumstance: they were "lettered" men, forming an elite group, while a majority of the three million remaining population was illiterate. Today's elected leaders do not have this or any other noteworthy skill making them uniquely qualified to lead us. Upon taking office, they do assume the circumstantial powers of their earliest predecessors, although without a similar landscape.

America's early architects and painters had the luxury of experimenting with the new and untested, because game and useful land were plentiful and freely accessible, forming natural shields for the citizenry against those unkind vulgarities, class distinction and privilege. Today's elected maintain as sacrosanct a muddled and fractured economic façade that can no longer render itself appropriate to scale, like fine, intricate carvings worn and covered in thick coats of paint. This refurbished patchwork is unable to meet the original's standards because all the past materials and conditions essential to its carefree and uncluttered design are no longer readily available.

Continued and expansive commercialization of historically essential needs has altered the economic landscape, making individual opportunity to fulfill basic needs today more privileged than an unfettered human effort. The latter was in the beginning of this nation (except for slaves and Indians) a silent assumption of reality. Rich or poor, educated or not, one's quality of life opportunities could be realized to at least a basic but essential degree through one's unobstructed effort. That reality is heralded loudly in the U.S. Declaration of Independence's "pursuit of happiness," although now that phrase is a faint echo. America's past abundance, and not early government leadership, made economic justice for most an obtainable aspiration.

Even in the first half of the twentieth century, America's economic prowess was buttressed by stretches of ocean and cheap physical labor. The first was an economic protector from a world in turmoil; the latter, an agrarian lifestyle replaced by newer urban plantations called office pools and factories offering services and shaping materials for domestic and foreign consumption, where many hands were needed to make one unit of product. Our new era of business globalization and technology has rendered old assumptions and generalizations impractical given contemporary labor, consumption, and production realities.

Today's commercialization requires a matrix of pre-qualifiers that prohibits some from entering into quality-of-life opportunities, but more significantly, inadequate money means inadequate living fulfillment, more personal uncertainty, and life stress. Most of us do not build or buy homes, hunt or grow food. Instead, we purchase mortgages, shop at markets, pay with credit cards, use devices instead of manual labor to complete tasks, and so forth. An earthquake, tornado, or other natural occurrence can be life-changing, a commonly-viewed reality that mobilizes society to provide aid. But economics is not a phenomenon of nature, nor is it a science. A person unable to manage their economic affairs because money is lacking is merely an invisible person except to a few. Even when such persons are tallied together, that sum, though critical, is an unobserved mass to most

Afterthought

in society, growing undetected and unproductively until the whole of a society succumbs to a crippling paralysis. Any nation's economic prosperity and growth was and is today irrelevant, if that same welfare to individuals and businesses is compromised because inadequate resource and trade opportunities exist. Recall the Great Depression.

The fundamental issue for government is not whether products are being bought and sold or jobs are available. Rather, it is the question of what government must do, given narrow arbitrary motives and misguided policies may inhibit access to the fulfillment of an individual's basic human right—opportunity for betterment. A chair to sit in or a television to watch is of little comfort if adequate shelter cannot be had. Conducting business and working for hire, whether at the behest of kings, merchants, or producers in all civilizations throughout world history, were adjuncts to the human experience and not the reason for one's existence.

U.S. leaders at all government levels need to rethink the economic circumstances of today by first doing as this country's framers did: start from scratch. New economic philosophy, policy, and management practices are urgent. Because the longer current circumstances persist, imbalances in economic opportunities will grow larger. Forcing choices to become more an act of desperation than circumspection. Thereby, raising the chances of bigger unattended consequences. As with the new job interview, those existing economic policies, laws, and regulations cannot act as the foundation for building something new when preexisting facts forming their basis have irreversibly changed. The fact that money doesn't grow on trees is a more significant cliché today because governmental distribution and regulation of money has been privately commercialized to such extent. It has lost its uniquely useful purpose as a medium for exchange or alternate barter method, becoming a commodity in its own right and limiting further the availability of circumstances for more and more businesses and persons by effectively destroying true value and real time comparisons in pricing and earnings transactions.

The land of milk and honey is gone. Most Americans have to satisfy their quality-of-life concerns through commercial enterprise opportunities. Make no mistake, it is not a responsibility or an inclination for businesses to create jobs and hire because persons need work or, for that matter, to pay their workers sufficient income. Further, commercialism is here to stay and should, because overall it can accelerate opportunities within the limit of a spatial boundary. However, the continual shrinking of the horn of plenty and expanding commercialization means governmental leaders must first abandon any preconceived economic assumptions. If there are no more free lunches, then who should eat when income is wanting: the lucky, the favored, the able, or the needy? Whether a government becomes bigger or smaller is irrelevant; what is needed is a more perfect economic system.

How governmental leadership is arrived at is a less critical matter than the act of governance itself. King Solomon, where art thou? The economy must be governed not by the "snowman philosophy" of yesteryear: little heads placed on top of big bellies, victimized by erstwhile climates, where the belly is merely an unanimated platform, a populace supporting a do-nothing head. Picture the snowman's head, a well-guarded privilege appropriating its prominence and more, regardless of effort. Today, as governance fails in its responsibility and power to properly manage and balance the economic climate for enterprises and individuals, economic futures awaiting most of us may be a series of stagnant puddles.

Are the men and women who lead us today intellectually inept, creatively dull, or overwhelmed by the enormity of their workload? Consider this candid admission by a U.S. Congressman: "My dear man, do you really think we have the time to read, let alone analyze, any good amount of the volume of information that comes to us for review and voting? You just have no idea how things really work around here." The latter would seem a fairer assessment, and if that is the case, is it not they that determine their work priorities? As required, can't they change their work focus, structure, policies, and procedures to do a better job of governing? Haven't our leaders given themselves personal opportunities for quality-of-life benefits beyond that of most citizens? The difference today is that governments must have individuals at their helms that are job-qualified beyond political and public relations activities. Governance can no longer be a laissez-faire entitlement by elected leadership.

I believe that a new economic system for the United States is needed and achievable. However, I also believe that sovereign nation economies are a detriment to developing even greater economic benefits for each nation and all humanity. The United States has been testing what will probably be the last great social experiment by a single nation—achieving a vibrantly diverse economic one. Despite some notable problems, like unilaterally showing that armaments for social/economic change are like using bandages to cure cancer, this noble experiment continues. Ironically, businesses from many nations have transformed into multinationals and have already begun scripting humanity's economic future on a global plane without any shots being fired between nations. For anyone, anywhere, to pretend a new global economic system does not have credibility or is too far-fetched of an idea would be foolish. Money, benefits, retirement, cost, price, resources, and so forth have coalesced, becoming humanity's new earth. All nations have lost their independent or self-reliant economies forever. Most notably, this new, artificial earth, unlike genuine earth, is no longer easily visible to the eye or firm under foot, making individual advancement across this landscape that is increasingly cluttered with others' economic injuries an uninspiring and unconfident trek for most.

Afterthought

Will the leading industrial nations join with others to craft a world economic system that maximizes the migration of individual passions, work skills, and experience throughout the earth? Will they speak to their citizenry, telling them the time is upon us where natural resources, personal resources, and quality-of-life opportunities can be more expansive beyond familiar borders, and they are world citizens as much as they are nationals? Will nations as a whole regulate the earth's natural resources so that those who fashion goods and services can enjoy profits without such enterprises controlling or limiting access to those resources? Or will leaders be ashamed to hold public dialogue openly, each fearing some will call him or her unpatriotic? We make our history, and economics is a human activity, a way of living. Its reality will not be found in mathematics, symbols, and formulas of theoretical textbooks and minds. There is little needing discovery or testing to bring this to fruition; generations and nations have been working this notion in many ways for millennia. Today, some nations have huge, underutilized and underdeveloped populations, resources, services, and products, while others have advanced methods and learned operators.

This postscript has attempted to frame the premise for employment as a quality-of-life issue in search of a new economic platform. In the U.S., viewpoints on interest, taxation, statehood, regionalism, insurance, a uniform world money standard, the Federal Reserve System, and more are being discussed and written about in many circles. Four fundamental conditions must be apart of a new global economy:

- A new global currency and coinage system must replace that of sovereigns'
- The practice of commercial interest dealing in money must be abolished
- All privately held insurance (life, casualty, health, business) operations must end and insurance coverage must continue via administration by a global governmental body
- There must be global wage and salary standards for industries' workers

For example, the application of interest on money—not to be confused with loan, credit and stock purchasing transactions—indicates how deeply business and individual welfare can be impeded by just one aspect of an overall economy.

A media commentary mentioned that two leading manufacturers reported that their financial arms were their most profitable operations. Obviously, the interest earned by them, regardless of the avenues by which derived, amounts to net zero in product sale gains. So, they each made profit through money trade. Or did they? Interest paid and earned in an economy is an additional price added to all products and services exchanged in the marketplace. Not just a price per transaction, but an accumulated price added to each succeeding transaction from the beginning of its introduction in the business cycle (which means decades in some cases). In other words, these two producers have earned interest by the front door, but the wages, materials, and other costs of doing business with interest have also been leaving by the back door for a very long time, not to mention that buyers of their products are entertaining the same scenario. This forms a quandary, so complicated and convoluted that a computer couldn't separate the inflated cost that monetary interest has added to all services and products exchanged in the economy. Interest is a magic show in which the world is fooled and applauds the moment. Commercial interest was introduced centuries ago, but its longevity is due to its common acceptance. Causing trade in the world to be supplanted by methods in exchange versus value in exchange. It adds nothing to the value of tangible products and services except distortions, and those who realize earnings from it have unfair advantage over those that don't, making participation more a mandatory than a voluntary affair—that's its trick. If one of those producers abandoned interest, then that business would be ruined, and if both of them did the same, then each would collapse. Without the influence of interest dealing in the world and other impediments, we would see trade activity accelerate, stock exchanges become more robust, and the supply and demand pendulum begin to swing smoothly in the community marketplace.

Looking at insurance as a commercial industry also demonstrates again how the public's treasury has been compromised. Why should insurance companies' earn profits by the redistribution of cash? By eliminating non-insurance related operations by executives, premium loadings, and commissions while creating a larger single group of policyholders (everyone is the potential risk pool) means lower insurance cost for everyone. The U.S. Postal Service sorts and delivers effectively millions of pieces of mail everyday for pennies. Insurance coverage provided by a single government entity would reduce individual premiums from dollars to pennies also.

Governmental leaders that can critically think are in a most formidable position to enact new economic principles, policies, and practices. Making price, and therefore expense, dependent on non-monetary supply and demand forces would be a sensible first step. Accommodating and increasing investments in those businesses that produce tangible goods and services are essential, rather than being appreciative to currency redistribution businesses, those that make money, yet produce naught. This would lessen the personal burden of unemployment and retirement periods by eliminating price and cost premiums in the economic marketplace. Making the opportunity of profitability and the acquiring of assets a necessity of effort/work and perceptions for all, means fluctuations related to economic matters will be smaller and fewer for everyone over time.

A single economic system with worker wage parity among nations can draw businesses and workers at various levels more easily to create expanding market potentials. This can stimulate, promote, and develop a better quality of life for businesses and people locally. In turn, local markets and businesses growth can spin off, forming larger connections for more quality-of-life opportunities broadly. It means that trade exchange between national governments will not be on the basis of currency evaluations, but negotiated resource needs.

Do governmental leaders have the wisdom, guts and tenacity to step outside their social comfort zones and those relationships of self-aggrandizement? Can they lead humanity towards a more stable and beneficial economy? Have they forgotten that, like every other person who earns a livelihood, they too are obliged to perform at their best for those who are paying for their services—leadership? A wise and just government values progress by giving positive recognition to all aspects of reasonableness, while that which is closer to childishness and tyranny guards privilege for the few by ridicule and obstruction. Government leaders show maturity and integrity by doing their best at public stewardship, accepting and showing responsibility for finding answers and making those decisions that best serve all the public's welfare. From tribal groups to nation states, through new business technologies and transportation, humanity has shrunk geography and time as former barriers to managing global trade opportunities. We can literally stand anywhere on this planet within a day and communicate with one another across its expanse in seconds with relative convenience.

Unlike the world of business, government is fiduciary, with a much larger sphere of influence and far broader concerns and consequences. Therefore, it must be selfless to be fair and effective. From humanity's beginning, trade has led and drawn diverse people together despite differences in religion, language, and culture. The United Nations is the only international organization on earth that can readily garner the attention and begin the re-organization of nations into a single economic sphere: separate nations with only one economic system serving all. What nations will begin the work? A diverse humanity, realizing individual purposes and possibilities through expanded quality-of-life opportunities, can be our common economic effort. Development and promotion of one's nation as empire is a barbaric concept without human dignity and modern rationale. It is not important that the United States or any nation be the greatest but that the greatest opportunities for a better quality of life exist for all humanity.

Shortly before this book went to print, Hurricane Katrina wreaked destruction and tragedy upon the United States. As my wife and I watched news unfolding, a reporter asked a most senior federal official the following question: "Sir, how will we (the U.S.) manage to pay for this massive recovery effort, considering our war in Iraq?" The response: "We have more than enough resources to do both." I turned to my wife and sarcastically remarked, "That's reassuring isn't it?" She snapped, "It stands to reason. We can print as much money as we want. It's not like we have to find it." A uniform world fiat monetary system is not as farfetched as one might think either. God Willing.

Do you see a square on this page? Learned thought patterns can obstruct adaptive thinking. That's the problem in having a mental set. In reality, there are no sides present, except in our mind's eye.

References by Chapter

"Why Employment?" Chapter 1

Black, H. C. (1979). *Black's Law Dictionary Fifth Edition*. Saint Paul, Minn.: West Publishing Co.

Campbell, J., Trapnell, P. D., Heine, S. J.; et. al. (1996). "Self-concept clarity: Measurement, Personality Correlates, and Cultural Boundaries." *Journal of Personality and Social Psychology*, 70, 141-156.

Cialdini, R. B. (1993). *Influence: The Psychology of Persuasion*. New York: Quill/Morrow.

de Rivera, J. (1989). "Comparing Experiences Across Cultures: Shame and Guilt in America and Japan." *Hiroshima Forum for Psychology*, 14, 13-20.

Glew, D. J., O'Leary-Kelly, A. M., Griffin, R. W., & Van Fleet, D. D. (1995). "Participation in Organizations: A Preview of the Issues and Proposed Framework for Future Analysis." *Journal of Management*, 21, 395-421.

Gross, M. L. (1962). *The Brain Watchers*. New York: Random House.

Hoffman, L. R. & Maier, N. R. F. (1961). "Quality and Acceptance of Problem Solutions by Members of Homogenous and Heterogeneous Groups." *Journal of Abnormal and Social Psychology*, 62, 401-407.

Hui, C. H., Yee, C. and Eastman, K. L. (1995). "The Relationship between Individualism-Collectivism and Job Satisfaction." *Applied Psychology: An International Review*, 44, 276-282.

Isaac, W. (1992). "The Ladder of Inference." Working Paper, MIT. Center for Organizational Learning. In P. M. Senge, (1990). *The Fifth Discipline*. New York: Currency Doubleday.

Janis, I. L. (1972). *Victims of Groupthink: A Psychological Study of Foreign Policy Decisions and Fiascoes.* Boston: Houghton Mifflin.

Jerdee, T. H. (1966). "Work-Group versus Individual Differences in Attitude." *Journal of Applied Psychology,* 50, 431-433.

Jones, E. E. and Nisbett, R. E. (1972). *The Actor and the Observer: Divergent Perceptions of the Causes of Behavior.* Morristown, NJ: General Learning Press.

Kahn, R. L. and Katz, D. (1953). "Leadership Practices in Relation to Productivity and Morale." In D. Cartwright, and A. Zander. (eds.) *Group Dynamics.* Evanston, IL: Row, Peterson and Co., 616.

Kashima, Y., Yamaguchi, S., Kim, U.; et. al. (1995). "Culture, Gender and Self: A Perspective from Individualism-Collectivism Research." *Journal of Personality and Social Psychology,* 69, 925-937.

McKelvey, W. W. (1969). "Expectational Noncomplimentarity and Style of Interaction between Professional and Organization." *Administrative Science Quarterly,* 14(1), 21-32.

Mullen, B. and Cooper, C. (1994). "The Relation between Group Cohesiveness and Performance: An Integration." *Psychological Bulletin,* 115, 210-227.

Porter, L. W., Steers, R. M., Mowday, R. T. and Boulian, P. V. (1974). "Organizational Commitment, Job Satisfaction, and Turnover among Psychiatric Technicians." *Journal of Applied Psychology,* 59, 603-609.

Triandis, H. C. (1996). "The Psychological Measurement of Cultural Syndromes." *American Psychologist,* 51, 407-415.

Vroom, V. (1964). *Work and Motivation.* New York: John Wiley and Sons, Inc.

"Business Sense," Chapter 2

Bennis, W. (1989). *Why Leaders Can't Lead: The Unconscious Conspiracy Continues.* Los Angeles: Jossey-Bass Publishers.

Collins, B. E. and Brief, D. A. (1995). "Using Person-Perception Vignette Methodologies to Uncover the Symbolic Meanings of Teacher Behaviors in the Milgram Paradigm." *Journal of Social Issues,* 51, 89-106.

Hochschild, A. (1983). *The Managed Heart.* Berkeley: University of California Press.

Kahn, J. S., Wolfe, D. M., Quinn, R. P., Snoek, J. D., and Rosenthal, R. A. (1964). *Organizational Stress: Studies in Role Conflict and Ambiguity*. New York: Wiley.

Milgram, S. (1974). *Obedience to Authority: An Experimental View*. New York: Harper Row.

"Interviewer Concerns," Chapter 3

Baron, R. A. (1993). "Interviewers' Moods and Evaluations of Job Applicants: The Role of Applicant Qualifications." *Journal of Applied Social Psychology*, 23, 253-271.

Berman, J. S. and Kenny, D. A. (1976). "Correlational Bias in Observer Ratings." *Journal of Personality and Social Psychology*, 34, 263-273.

Birdwhistell, R. L. (1970). *Kinesics and Context: Essays on Body Motion Communication*. Philadelphia: University of Pennsylvania Press.

Broadbent, D. E. (1971). *Decision and Stress*. New York: Academic Press.

Broadbent, D. E. (1979). "Human Performance and Noise." In C. M. Harris (ed.), *Handbook of Noise Control*. New York: McGraw-Hill.

Cappella, J. N. and Palmer, M. T. (1990). "Attitude Similarity, Relational History, and Attraction: The Mediating Effects of Kinesic and Vocal Behavior." *Communication Monographs*, 57, 161-183.

Forgas, J. P. (1998). "On Being Happy and Mistaken: Mood Effects on the Fundamental Attribution Error." *Journal of Personality and Social Psychology*, 75, 318-331.

Gaugler, B. B., Rosenthal, D. B., Thorton, G. C., and Bentson, C. (1987). "Meta-Analysis of Assessment Center Validity." *Journal of Applied Psychology*, 72, 493-511.

Gottfredson, L. S. (1986). "The G Factor in Employment" (Special Issue). *Journal of Vocational Behavior*, 29(3).

Harrison, R. (1965). "Nonverbal Communication: Exploration into Time, Space, Action, and Object." In J.H. Campbell and H.W. Helper (1965) *Dimensions in Communication*, eds. Belmont, CA.: Wadsworth Publishing Co., Inc., 101.

Hatfield, E., Cacioppo, J. T. and Rapson, R. L. (1994). *Emotional Contagion*. New York: Cambridge University Press.

Huffcutt, A. I., and Arthur, W. (1994). "Hunter and Hunter (1984) Revisited: Interview Validity for Entry-Level Jobs." *Journal of Applied Psychology*, 79, 184-190.

Hunter, J. E. (1986). "Cognitive Ability, Cognitive Aptitudes, Job Knowledge and Job Performance." *Journal of Vocational Behavior*, 29, 340-362.

Ichheiser, G. (1970). *Appearance and Realities*. San Francisco: Jossey-Bass, Inc.

Kahnemann, D., and Tversky, A. (1973). "On the Psychology of Prediction." *Psychological Review*, 80, 237-251.

Kloman, William (Autumn 1967). "E. T. Hall and the Human Space Bubble." *Horizon*, 9, 43.

Luchins, A. S. (1957). "Experimental Attempts to Minimize the Impact of First Impressions." In C. Hovland (ed.), *The Order of Presentation in Persuasion*. New Haven: Yale University Press, 63-75.

Manz, W. and Lueck, H. (1968). "Influence of Wearing Glasses on Personality Ratings: Cross-Cultural Validation of an Old Experiment." *Perceptual and Motor Skills*, 27, 704.

McDaniel, M. A., Whetzel, D. L., Schmidt, F. L., and Maurer, S. D. (1994). "The Validity of Employment Interviews: A Comprehensive Review and Meta-Analysis." *Journal of Applied Psychology*, 79, 599-616.

Nisbett, R. E. and Ross, L. D. (1980). "Human Inference: Strategies and Shortcomings of Social Judgement." *Century Psychology Series*. Englewood Cliffs, NJ: Prentice-Hall, Inc.

Rosenthal, R. (1974). "Body Talk and Tone of Voice—The Language Without Words." *Psychology Today*, September 1974, 64-68.

Ross, R. S. and Ross, M. G. (1982). *Relating and Interacting*. Englewood Cliffs, NJ: Prentice-Hall, Inc.

Schneider, D. J. (1973). "Implicit Personality Theory: A Review." *Psychological Bulletin*, 73, 294-309.

Siegman, A. W. and Reynolds, M. (1982). "Interviewer-Interviewee Non-Verbal Communications: An Interactional Approach." In M. Davis (ed.), *Interaction Rhythms: Periodicity in Communicative Behavior* (249-278). New York: Human Sciences Press.

Snyder, M. (1979). "Self-Monitoring Processes." In L. Berkowitz (ed.), *Advances in Experimental Social Psychology*, vol. 12. New York: Academic Press.

Snyder, M. and Swann, W. (1978). "Behavioral Confirmation in Social Interaction: From Social Perception to Social Reality." *Journal of Experimental Social Psychology*, 14, 148-162.

"Preparing Interview Content," Chapter 4

Mager, R. F. (1997). *Goal Analysis*. 3rd Ed. Atlanta: The Center for Effective Performance, Inc.

Osburn, H. G., Timmreck, C., and Bigby, D. (1981). "Effect of Dimensional Relevance on Accuracy of Simulated Hiring Decisions by Employment Interviewers." *Journal of Applied Psychology*, 66, 159-165.

"Talent and Bumps in the Dark," Chapter 5

Amabile, Teresa M. (1983). *The Social Psychology of Creativity*. New York: Springer-Verlag.

Getzels, J. W. and Jackson, P. W. (1962). *Creativity and Intelligence*. New York: John Wiley and Sons, Inc.

Ghiselli, E. (1966). *The Validity of Occupational Aptitude Tests*. New York: Wiley.

King, P. M., and Kitchener, K. S. (1994). *Developing Reflective Judgement: Understanding and Promoting Intellectual Growth and Critical Thinking in Adolescents and Adults*. San Francisco: Jossey-Bass.

Kitchener, K. S.; Lynch, C. L.; Fischer, K. W.; Wood, P. K. (1993). "Developmental Range of Reflective judgement: The Effect of Contextual Support and Practice on Developmental Stage." *Developmental Psychology*, 31, 95-104.

Kitchener, K. S. and King, P. M. (1990). "The Reflective Judgement Model: Ten Years of Research." In M. L. Commons (ed.), *Models and Methods in the Study of Adolescent and Adult Thought, Vol. 2: Adult Development*. Westport, CT: Greenwood Press.

McCrea, Robert R. (1987). "Creativity, Divergent Thinking, and Openness to Experience." *Journal of Personality and Social Psychology*, 52, 1258-1265.

Schank, Roger C. (1988). *The Creative Attitude*. New York: Macmillan.

Walberg, H. J., Rasher, S. P. and Parkerson, J. (1980). "Childhood and Eminence." *Journal of Creative Behavior* 13, 225-231.

White, R. K. (1931). "The Versatility of Genius." *Journal of Social Psychology*, 2, 460-489.

Wigdor, A. K., and Garner, W. R. (Eds.). (1982). *Ability Testing: Uses, Consequences, and Controversies.* Washington, DC: National Academy Press.

"Applicant Beware," Chapter 6

Barber, A. E. and Roehling, M. V. (1993). "Job Postings and the Decision to Interview: A Verbal Protocol Analysis." *Journal of Applied Psychology*, 78, 845-856.

Covington, M. V. and Omelich, C. L. (1979). "Effort: The Double Edged Sword in School Achievement." *Journal of Educational Psychology*, 71, 169-182.

Goffman, E. (1959). *The Presentation of Self in Everyday Life.* Garden City, NY: Doubleday.

Terman, L. M. and Oden, M. H. (1959). *Genetic Studies of Genius, Vol.5: The Gifted Group at Mid-Life.* Stanford, CA: Stanford University Press.

Tullar, W. L., Mullins, T. W. and Caldwell, S. A. (1979). "Effects of Interview Length and Applicant Quality on Interview Decision Time." *Journal of Applied Psychology*, 64, 669-674.

"Session Essentials," Chapter 8

Olson, D. R. (1986). "Intelligence and Literacy: The Relationship between Intelligence and the Technologies of Representation and Communication." In R. J. Sternberg and R. K Wagner (eds.). *Practical Intelligence.* New York: Cambridge University Press.

"Putting It All Together," Chapter 9

Adkins, C. L., Russell, C. J., and Werbel, J. D. (1994). "Judgements of Fit in the Selection Process: The Role of Work Value Congruence." *Personnel Psychology*, 47, 605-623.

Anderson, J. R. (1987). "Skill Acquisition: Compilation of Weak-Method Problem Solutions." *Psychological Review*, 94, 192-210.

Klemp, G. O. and McClelland, D.C. (1986). "What Characterizes Intelligent Functioning Among Senior Managers?" In R. J. Sternberg and R. K Wagner (eds.). *Practical Intelligence*. New York: Cambridge University Press.

Kintsch, W. (1989). "The Role of Knowledge in Discourse Comprehension: A Construction-Integration Model." *Psychological Review*, 95, 163-182.

Scribner, S. (1986). "Thinking in Action: Some Characteristics of Practical Thought." In R. J. Sternberg and R. K Wagner (eds.). *Practical Intelligence*. New York: Cambridge University Press.

Sternberg, R. J. (1988). *The Triarchic Mind: A New Theory of Human Intelligence*. NY: Viking.

Sternberg, R. J.; Wagner, R. K.; Williams, W. M. and Horvath, J. A. (1995). "Testing Common Sense." *American Psychologist*, 50, 912-927.

Sternberg, R. J.; Wagner, R. K. and Okagaki, L. (1993). "Practical Intelligence: The Nature and Role of Tacit Knowledge and Its Acquisition." In P. Ackerman, R. J. Sternberg and R. Glaser (eds), *Individual differences*. New York: Freeman.

Wallach, M. A. and Kogan, N. (1965). *Modes of Thinking in Young Children*. New York: Holt, Rinehart and Winston, Inc.

Index

A

Adkins, C.L. 67
Amabile, T.M. 68
Anderson, J.R. 66
applicant's readiness
    importance of 95
applicant's responses
    interviewer considerations 101
applicant's
    responsibilities 76, 78, 92, 95
Arthur, W. 51
attitude 27
    group comformity 88
    interview assessing 127
    morale 26
    a bias 130

B

Barber, A.E. 80
Baron, R.A. 46
Bennis, W. 38
Berman, J.S. 49
Bigby, D. 58
big money 18
Birdwhistell, R.L. 46
Brief, D.A. 34
Broadbent, D.E. 51
brown-nosing 83
business organization
    defined 29
business process
    aspects of 9
    consistency 20

C

Campbell, J. 21
Cappella, J.N. 46
Cialdini, R.B. 20
civil servants 89
    run government 90
Collins, B.E. 34
competition 32
    market driven 32
competitors 33, 90
connective interview
    comparative highlights 118
    opposing view 125
connectivity
    to job 110

Copper, C. 16
Covington, M.V. 84
creativity
    versus intelligence 68
credentials 65
critical thinking 53, 116, 118
    characteristics 70, 71
    versus decision-making 74
customer loyalty 90

D

de Rivera, J. 21
diversity
    organizational need 56, 57

E

Eastman, K.L. 21
educated
    versus intelligent 68
elected officials
    appointees 58
    decision making 88
    job skill 89
    products 89
employee
    development 62, 79, 82
    probation 63
    retention 80, 129
employee's job success 37
employee satisfaction
    versus job satisfaction 37
employer's
    modern employment perspective 115
employer's
    determinants 112, 115
employment 15, 16
    archacic 14
    defined 14, 126, 128, 130
    misguided 16
    nesting 90
employment's
    climates 91
    focus 18
    intents 15
    perspective 93, 99
    unique arrangement 17, 18, 19, 34
employment condition 84
empowerment 82

F

first impressions 76
Forgas, J.P. 48

G

Garner, W.R. 67
Gaugler, B.B. 53
Getzels, J.W. 69
Ghiselli, E. 67
Glew, D.J. 19
goal analysis
  purpose 59
Goffman, E. 84
Gottfredson, L.S. 52
government 89
Gross, M. L. 22
groupthink 20
group identity
  illusionry 63

H

Harrison, R. 47
Hatfield, E. 46
hero
  defined 32
Hochschild, A. 30, 31
Hoffman, L.R. 20
Huffcutt, A.I. 51
Hui, C.H. 21
Human Performance Technology 2
  as assessment model 110
Hunter, J.E. 52

I

Ichheiser, G. 48
imagination 68
individual bias 74
informational
  relatedness 35
internal promotions
  versus hiring 125
interviewer(s)
  common viewpoints 43
  competencies 45
  critical impact 56
  etiquette 44
  influence mood 46
  inquiry 100, 103, 111
  natural biases 5
  role 21, 39, 45, 61
  situational control 6, 11
  traditional focus 42

interviewing process 2
  a standard 5
  not intuitive 13
  new requirement 55
  preparation 57
interviewing session
  applicant discomfort 38, 44
  duration of 98
  scheduling 97
  staggered 50
interview books 43
intimidation 47
involuntarily discharge 10
IQ
  job success 67
  test 68
Isaac, W. 27

J

Jackson, P.W. 69
Janis, I.L. 20
Jerdee, T.H. 26
job content 37, 88, 117
job context 88, 110
job description 61
job interview
  purpose 6
job interviewing
  defined 6
  erroneous concepts 6
job seeker's
  best option 10
  imperative 16
job titles
  misleading 56
Jones, E. E. 25

K

Kahn, J.S. 38
Kahn, R.L. 26
Kahneman, D. 49
Kashima, Y. 21
Katz, D. 26
Kenny, D.A. 49
kinesics 46
King, P.M. 71, 72
Kintsch, W. 67
Kitchener, K.S. 71, 72
Klemp, G.O. 117
Kloman, W. 47
knowledge
  declarative 67
  procedural 66

tacit 116
Kogan, N. 74

L

labor unions 91
leadership
   business attributes 83, 117
   military.. 83
   recognition of 82
   trainee 117
loyalty 26, 128
Luchins, A.S. 49
Lueck, H. 49

M

Mager, R.F. 59
Maier, N.R.F. 20
Manz, W. 49
McClelland, D.C. 117
McCrea, R. R. 68
McDaniel, M.A. 51
McKelvey, W.W. 20
Milgram, S. 34
military 31, 32, 83, 88, 105
mind games 78
mind reading.. 13, 37
motivation
   importance to employers 78
Mullen, B. 16

N

negotiating compensation 81
Nisbett, R.E. 25, 49

O

Oden, M.H. 79
Okagaki, L. 116
Olson, D.R. 101
Omelich, C.L. 84
organizational
   climate.. 91
   development 23, 24, 33, 90
   fit 38
Osburn, H.G. 58
over-qualified 79, 80

P

Palmer, M.T. 46
personality
   defined 24
   testing 22
   versus a behavior 22

personality judgments
   low validity... 22
personality traits... 13, 68
personnel management.................................... 20
political parties... 32, 91
Porter, L.W. 18
positioning... 17, 18
position profile
   example of 60
   statement clauses 59
   steps in making... 61
      aids perception 101
      basis 74
      before interviewing................................... 98
      the interview foundation 57
poverty.. 81
power 82, 88
prepackaged interview material....................... 13
probationary period... 63
psychologist(s).. 53

R

Reynolds, M. 46
Roehling, M.V. 80
role
   authoirity 83
   distinctive 32
   image interviews 78
   interviewer's knowledge of 50
   involuntary 24
   management 125
   self-identity 85
   set   37
role playing
   effect employer diversity 57
Rosenthal, R. 47
Ross, L.D. 49
Ross, M.G. 47
Ross, R.S. 47
Russell, C.L. 67

S

Schank, R.C. 68
Schneider, D.J. 49
selective attention..................................... 51, 112
   individual 52
self-employed 84
   distinction 93
Siegman, A.W. 46
Snyder, M. 49
sports 88, 105
Sternberg, R.J. 116
structured interviews 51

    biographical/behaviorial 52
    critical incident... 52
    situational.. 52
Swann, W. 49
synchrony... 46

T

teaming 31
team sports 32
Terman, L.M. 79
the gifted 70, 79
the work
    defines role 56
    two types of 31
thinking
    as process 68
Timmreck, C. 58
traditional interview
    not process 41, 43
        hampers interviewers 14
        mask creativity 68
training 38, 70, 95
transparency 14, 127
Triandis, H.C. 21
trust
    active 26
    applicant failure 95
Tullar, W.L. 78
Tversky, A. 49

U

untrained interviewer(s) 47, 49, 53, 65

V

Vroom, V. 16

W

Wagner, R.K. 116
Walberg, H.J. 70
Wallach, M.A. 74
Werbel, J.D. 67
White, R.K. 70
Wigdor, A.K. 67
work
    strategy 33
work group 20
    as product 32

Y

Yee, C. 21

Printed in the United States
105955LV00006B/197/A